MACMILLAN MASTER GUIDES
HENRY IV PART I
BY WILLIAM SHAKESPEARE

HELEN MORRIS

with an Introduction by
HAROLD BROOKS

MACMILLAN

First edition 1986

Published by
MACMILLAN EDUCATION LTD
Houndmills, Basingstoke, Hampshire RG21 2XS
and London
Companies and representatives
throughout the world

Typeset in Great Britain by
TEC SET, Sutton, Surrey

Printed in Hong Kong

ISBN 0-333-39770-3 Pbk
ISBN 0-333-39771-1 Pbk export

MACMILLAN MASTER GUIDES

PLEASE DO NOT WRITE IN THIS BOOK

Also published by Macmillan

MASTERING ENGLISH LITERATURE R. Gill
MASTERING ENGLISH LANGUAGE S. H. Burton
MASTERING ENGLISH GRAMMAR S. H. Burton

WORK OUT SERIES

WORK OUT ENGLISH LANGUAGE ('O' level and GCSE) S. H. Burton
WORK OUT ENGLISH LITERATURE ('A' level) S. H. Burton

CONTENTS

GENERAL EDITOR'S PREFACE

The aim of the Macmillan Master Guides is to help you to appreciate the book you are studying by providing information about it and by suggesting ways of reading and thinking about it which will lead to a fuller understanding. The section on the writer's life and background has been designed to illustrate those aspects of the writer's life which have influenced the work, and to place it in its personal and literary context. The summaries and critical commentary are of special importance in that each brief summary of the action is followed by an examination of the significant critical points. The space which might have been given to repetitive explanatory notes has been devoted to a detailed analysis of the kind of passage which might confront you in an examination. Literary criticism is concerned with both the broader aspects of the work being studied and with its detail. The ideas which meet us in reading a great work of literature, and their relevance to us today, are an essential part of our study, and our Guides look at the thought of their subject in some detail. But just as essential is the craft with which the writer has constructed his work of art, and this is considered under several technical headings - characterisation, language, style and stagecraft.

The authors of these Guides are all teachers and writers of wide experience, and they have chosen to write about books they admire and know well in the belief that they can communicate their admiration to you. But you yourself must read and know intimately the book you are studying. No one can do that for you. You should see this book as a lamppost. Use it to shed light, not to lean against. If you know your text and know what it is saying about life, and how it says it, then you will enjoy it, and there is no better way of passing an examination in literature.

JAMES GIBSON

AN INTRODUCTION TO THE STUDY OF SHAKESPEARE'S PLAYS

A play as a work of art exists to the full only when performed. It must hold the audience's attention throughout the performance, and, unlike a novel, it can't be put down and taken up again. It is important to experience the play as if you are seeing it on the stage for the first time, and you should begin by reading it straight through. Shakespeare builds a play in dramatic units which may be divided into smaller subdivisions, or episodes, marked off by exits and entrances and lasting as long as the same actors are on the stage. Study it unit by unit.

The first unit provides the exposition which is designed to put the audience into the picture. In the second unit we see the forward movement of the play as one situation changes into another. The last unit in a tragedy or a tragical play will bring the catastrophe and in comedy – and some of the history plays – an unravelling of the complications, what is called a *dénouement*.

The onward movement of the play from start to finish is its progressive structure. We see the chain of cause and effect (the plot) and the progressive revelation and development of character. The people, their characters and their motives drive the plot forward in a series of scenes which are carefully planned to give variety of pace and excitement. We notice fast-moving and slower-moving episodes, tension mounting and slackening, and alternate fear and hope for the characters we favour. Full-stage scenes, such as stately councils and processions or turbulent mobs, contrast with scenes of small groups or even single speakers. Each of the scenes presents a deed or event which changes the situation. In performance, entrances and exits and stage actions are physical facts, with more impact than on the page. That impact Shakespeare relied upon, and we must restore it by an effort of the imagination.

Shakespeare's language is just as diverse. Quickfire dialogue is followed by long speeches, and verse changes to prose. There is a wide range of speech - formal, colloquial, dialect, 'Mummerset' and the broken English of foreigners, for example. Songs, instrumental music, and the noise of battle, revelry and tempest, all extend the range of dramatic expression. The dramatic use of language is enhanced by skilful stagecraft, by costumes, by properties such as beds, swords and Yorick's skull, by such stage business as kneeling, embracing and giving money, and by use of such features of the stage structure as the balcony and the trapdoor.

By these means Shakespeare's people are brought vividly to life and cleverly individualised. But though they have much to tell us about human nature, we must never forget that they are characters in a play, not in real life. And remember, they exist to enact the play, not the play to portray *them*.

Shakespeare groups his characters so that they form a pattern, and it is useful to draw a diagram showing this. Sometimes a linking character has dealings with each group. The pattern of persons belongs to the symmetric structure of the play, and its dramatic unity is reinforced and enriched by a pattern of resemblances and contrasts; for instance, between characters, scenes, recurrent kinds of imagery, and words. It is not enough just to notice a feature that belongs to the symmetric structure, you should ask what its relevance is to the play as a whole and to the play's ideas.

These ideas and the dramatising of them in a central theme, or several related to each other, are a principal source of the dramatic unity. In order to see what themes are present and important, look, as before, for pattern. Observe the place in it of the leading character. In tragedy this will be the protagonist, in comedy heroes and heroines, together with those in conflict or contrast with them. In *Henry IV Part I*, Prince Hal is being educated for kingship and has a correct estimate of honour, while Falstaff despises honour, and Hotspur makes an idol of it. Pick out the episodes of great intensity as, for example, in *King Lear* where the theme of spiritual blindness is objectified in the blinding of Gloucester, and, simimarly, note the emphases given by dramatic poetry as in Prospero's 'Our revels now are ended. . .' or unforgettable utterances such as Lear's 'Is there any cause in Nature that makes these hard hearts?' Striking stage-pictures such as that of Hamlet behind the King at prayer will point to leading themes, as will all the parallels and recurrences, including those of phrase and imagery. See whether, in the play you are studying, themes known to be favourites with Shakespeare are prominent, themes such as those of order and disorder, relationships disrupted by mistakes about identity, and appearance and reality. The latter were bound to fascinate Shakespeare, whose theatrical art worked by means of illusions which pointed beyond the surface of actual life to underlying truths. In looking at themes beware of attempts to make the play fit some orthodoxy a critic believes in - Freudian perhaps, or Marxist, or dogmatic Christian theology - and remember that its ideas, though they often have a bearing on ours, are Elizabethan.

Some of Shakespeare's greatness lies in the good parts he wrote for the actors. In his demands upon them, and the opportunities he provided, he bore their professional skills in mind and made use of their physical prowess, relished by a public accustomed to judge fencing and wrestling as expertly as we today judge football and tennis. As a member of the professional group of players called the Chamberlain's Men he knew each actor he was writing for. To play his women he had highly-trained boys. As paired heroines they were often contrasted, short with tall, for example, or one vivacious and enterprising, the other conventionally feminine.

Richard Burbage, the company's leading man, was famous as a great tragic actor, and he took leading roles in seven of Shakespeare's tragedies. Though each of the seven has its own distinctiveness, we shall find at the centre of all of them a tragic protagonist possessing tragic greatness, not just one 'tragic flaw' but a tragic vulnerability. He will have a character which makes him unfit to cope with the tragic situations confronting him, so that his tragic errors bring down upon him tragic suffering and finally a tragic catastrophe. Normally, both the suffering and the catastrophe are far worse than he can be said to deserve, and others are engulfed in them who deserve such a fate less or not at all. Tragic terror is aroused in us because, though exceptional, he is sufficiently near to normal humankind for his fate to remind us of what can happen to human beings like ourselves, and because we see in it a combination of inexorable law and painful mystery. We recognise the principle of cause and effect where in a tragic world errors return upon those who make them, but we are also aware of the tragic disproportion between cause and effect. In a tragic world you may kick a stone and start an avalanche which will destroy you and others with you. Tragic pity is aroused in us by this disproportionate suffering, and also by all the kinds of suffering undergone by every character who has won our imaginative sympathy. Imaginative sympathy is wider than moral approval, and is felt even if suffering does seem a just and logical outcome. In addition to pity and terror we have a sense of tragic waste because catastrophe has affected so much that was great and fine. Yet we feel also a tragic exaltation. To our grief the men and women who represented those values have been destroyed, but the values themselves have been shown not to depend upon success, nor upon immunity from the worst of tragic suffering and disaster.

Comedies have been of two main kinds, or cross-bred from the two. In critical comedies the governing aim is to bring out the absurdity or irrationality of follies and abuses, and make us laugh at them. Shakespeare's comedies often do this, but most of them belong primarily to the other kind – romantic comedy. Part of the romantic appeal is to our liking for suspense; they are dramas of averted threat, beginning in trouble and ending in joy. They appeal to the romantic senses of adventure and of wonder, and to complain that they are improbable is silly because the improbability, the marvellousness, is part of the pleasure. They dramatise stories of romantic love, accompanied by love doctrine - ideas and ideals of love. But they are plays in two tones, they are comic as well as romantic. There is often something to laugh at even in the love stories of the nobility and gentry, and just as there is high comedy in such incidents as the cross-purposes of the young Athenians in the wood, and Rosalind as 'Ganymede' teasing Orlando, there is always broad comedy for characters of lower rank. Even where one of the sub-plots has no effect on the main plot, it may take up a topic from it and present it in a more comic way.

What is there in the play to make us laugh or smile? We can distinguish many kinds of comedy it may employ. *Language* can amuse by its wit, or by absurdity, as in Bottom's malapropisms. Feste's nonsense-phrases, so fatuously admired by Sir Andrew, are deliberate, while his catechising of Olivia is clown-routine. Ass-headed Bottom embraced by the Fairy Queen is a *comic spectacle* combining costume and stage-business. His wanting to play every part is *comedy of character*. Phebe disdaining Silvius and in love with 'Ganymede', or Malvolia treating Olivia as though she had written him a love-letter is *comedy of situation*; the situation is laughably different from what Phebe or Malvolio supposes. A comic let-down or anticlimax can be devastating, as we see when Aragon, sure that he deserves Portia, chooses the silver casket only to find the portrait not of her but of a 'blinking idiot'. By *slapstick, caricature* or sheer *ridiculousness of situation*, comedy can be exaggerated into farce, which Shakespeare knows how to use on occasion. At the opposite extreme, before he averts the threat, he can carry it to the brink of tragedy, but always under control.

Dramatic irony is the result of a character or the audience anticipating an outcome which, comically or tragically, turns out very differently. Sometimes we foresee that it will. The speaker never foresees how ironical, looking back, the words or expectations will appear. When she says, 'A little water clears us of this deed' Lady Macbeth has no prevision of her sleep-walking words, 'Will these hands ne'er be clean?' There is irony in the way in which in all Shakespeare's tragic plays except *Richard II* comedy is found in the very heart of the tragedy. The Porter scene in *Macbeth* comes straight after Duncan's murder. In *Hamlet* and *Antony and Cleopatra* comic episodes lead into the catastrophe: the rustic Countryman brings Cleopatra the means of death, and the satirised Osric departs with Hamlet's assent to the fatal fencing match. The Porter, the Countryman and Osric are not mere 'comic relief', they contrast with the tragedy in a way that adds something to it, and affects our response.

A sense of the comic and the tragic is common ground between Shakespeare and his audience. Understandings shared with the audience are necessary to all drama. They include conventions, i.e. assumptions, contrary to what factual realism would demand, which the audience silently agrees to accept. It is, after all, by a convention, what Coleridge called a 'willing suspension of disbelief', that an actor is accepted as Hamlet. We should let a play teach us the convention it depends on. Shakespeare's conventions allow him to take a good many liberties, and he never troubles about inconsistencies that wouldn't trouble an audience. What matters to the dramatist is the effect he creates. So long as we are responding as he would wish, Shakespeare would not care whether we could say by what means he has made us do so. But to appreciate his skill, and get a fuller understanding of his play, we have to distinguish these means, and find terms to describe them.

If you approach the Shakespeare play you are studying bearing in mind what is said to you here, then you will respond to it more fully than before. Yet like all works of artistic genuis, Shakespeare's can only be analysed so far. His drama and its poetry will always have about them something 'which into words no critic can digest'.

HAROLD BROOKS

ACKNOWLEDGEMENTS

Cover illustration: *Anthony Quayle as Falstaff* by Sir William Dobell, courtesy of the governors of the Royal Shakespeare Theatre. The drawing of the Globe Theatre is by courtesy of Alec Pearson.

1 LIFE AND BACKGROUND

1.1 SHAKESPEARE: LIFE AND CAREER

We know that William Shakespeare was baptised on 26 April 1564. It is assumed that he was born on 23 April, so the greatest English poet and dramatist shares his birthday with the feast day of England's patron saint, St George.

He was born in the very heart of England, at Stratford-upon-Avon, in Warwickshire. His father, John Shakespeare, was a glover and leather-merchant, who became an alderman in 1565 and Bailiff (Mayor) of the town in 1568. After 1576 he apparently fell on hard times, for he did not pay his dues nor attend council meetings, and in 1586 was replaced on the council.

Shakespeare almost certainly attended the grammar school in the town, the King's New School, still to be seen in Church Street, which had well-qualified masters; but there is no evidence that he enjoyed it. Schoolboys in the plays are usually miserable; they sigh, whine, cry, are peevish, go reluctantly to, and hurry quickly away from, school. Schoolmasters are figures of fun. Armado in *Love's Labour's Lost* asks Holofernes, 'Monsieur, are you not lettered?' and the cheeky page Moth answers 'Yes, yes; he teaches boys the hornbook [a sheet showing the alphabet]. What is a, b, spelt backwards with the horn on his head?' 'Ba' is the answer – Holofernes is a muttonhead (V.i.49). In *The Merry Wives of Windsor* the comic Welsh schoolmaster questions little William in the words of Lyly's *Grammar*, which was presumably Shakespeare's textbook, in a short scene whose only purpose seems to be to mock schooling (IV.i).

It is not known what Shakespeare did when he left school; possibly he worked in his father's business as an apprentice. There is in the plays a great deal about leather, its varieties and qualities and uses, hides of oxen and horses, calf-skin, sheep-skin, lamb-skin, fox-skin, dog-skin, deerskin and cheveril. But this he might have picked up as a boy at home, and Shakespeare also knows a great deal about other trades and professions, and cannot have been apprenticed to them all.

In November 1582 he married in some haste, after only one calling of banns, Anne Hathaway, who was seven or eight years older than he was. In May 1583 their first child, Susanna, was born. In February 1585 they had twins, named Hamnet and Judith after friends of the family.

No one knows what Shakespeare did during the next seven years. He vanishes from view and reappears in London, as a playwright. His three plays about Henry VI must have been staged by 1592, because a pamphlet of that date, *Pierce Pennilesse* by Thomas Nashe, contains a compliment to *Henry VI Part I*, saying that the death of Talbot on the stage had drawn 'tears of ten thousand spectators at least (at severall times)'.

There is also an attack on Shakespeare by the playwright Robert Greene, in a posthumous pamphlet published in the same year. He wrote about an 'upstart Crow, beautified with our feathers, that with his *Tiger's heart wrapped in a player's hide* supposes he is as well able to bombast out a blank verse as the best of you, and being an absolute Johannes factotum [Jack-of-all trades] is in his own conceit the only Shake-scene in a country'. This is unmistakably directed at Shakespeare, 'Johannes factotum' because he was both writer and actor, and it parodies his description of Queen Margaret in *Henry VI Part III*, 'O tiger's heart wrapped in a woman's hide'. Greene, who died in poverty, was a University Wit and resented a grammar school playwright who was also an actor and a success. Greene was dead, but evidently friends of Shakespeare tackled the publisher of the pamphlet, Henry Chettle. He made a handsome apology, saying that Shakespeare's manners were as accomplished as his writing, and that many worthy gentlemen had reported him an honourable man and an excellent writer.

In 1593 and 1594 plague struck London and the theatres were closed. Shakespeare turned to poetry for a living, and published two long narrative poems, *Venus and Adonis* and *The Rape of Lucrece*, the only works that he himself saw through the press. It was the custom of poets to dedicate their books to a nobleman, hoping for a gift in return. Elizabethans had a cult of fame, and longed to be remembered after death; one way to have your name remembered was to have it printed on a book. Whatever the Earl of Southampton gave to Shakespeare for the two poems which were dedicated to him, he has been handsomely repaid; no one would remember him now if his name did not appear in front of Shakespeare's poems.

When the theatres opened again in 1594 Shakespeare was a member of the Lord Chamberlain's company of actors, the 'Lord Chamberlain's Men'. He was not a mere 'hired man' with a salary, but a 'sharer', owner of shares in the company, and getting a proportionate share of the profits. He was also their 'attached poet', writing exclusively for them two or three plays a year. There were no copyright laws to protect authors; once published, a play could be acted by anyone who wished. So it was only when necessity forced them – perhaps plague shutting the theatres, or bankruptcy, or the company breaking up – that plays appeared in print in the 1590s. Sometimes a hard-up actor might write down what he remembered of a play, and sell it to a printer. Often his own part would be word perfect, and the scenes he had appeared in fairly accurate, but the rest very sketchy. Because the companies guarded their scripts so jealously, only a very small proportion of plays have survived; of the 215 plays which the Admiral's Men acted from June 1594 to March 1603 only 15 now exist.

About half of Shakespeare's plays appeared in his lifetime, singly, in books called from their size 'Quartos'. There is no evidence that he was interested in having his plays read, or had anything to do with these publications. When he himself published his poems, they had a minimum of printers' errors, only two in the 1194 lines of *Venus and Adonis*, and three in the 1855 lines of *The Rape of Lucrece*. Many of the Quartos of his plays which appeared in Shakespeare's lifetime were highly imperfect, with inaccurate text and lots of missing lines. The Quartos are so badly printed that battalions of scholars have made it their life-work to try to discover the correct text. They could not have been seen through the press by the same man who proof-read the poems. Professor G. E. Bentley, the greatest living authority on the Elizabethan and Jacobean theatre, has calculated that the rate of printers' errors in the Quartos is one hundred times that in the poems.

Also, each of the poems had an elaborate dedication, but not one of the Quartos has a dedication, an author's preface, or an address to the reader. They contain only the bare speeches, with a very few stage directions, and do not have even a list of *dramatis personae*, the people in the play. Other Jacobean dramatists, including Thomas Dekker, John Marston, Thomas Middleton and Shakespeare's friend Ben Jonson, apparently did want their plays to be read, and published them with dedications and addresses to the reader. But it seems that Shakespeare wanted his works only to be acted. Many fascinating modern critics rely entirely on fine points of comparison, or repeated images, or on poetic subtleties which no audience could possibly pick up in the theatre. We must always remember that *Henry IV Part I* is a *play*.

Shakespeare's complete works first appeared in 1623, seven years after his death. They were collected into what is called the First Folio (F1) by two of his friends, members of the company, John Heminges and Henry Condell. Of these 36 plays, 18 were printed for the first time, including some of the very best, *Macbeth*, *As You Like It*, *Twelfth Night*, *The Tempest*, *Antony and Cleopatra*, and *Othello*.

Heminges and Condell knew how bad the Quartos were. In their preface they write that they wish to replace 'stolen and surreptitious copies, maimed and deformed', and that they collected the plays 'without ambition either of self-profit or fame; only to keep the memory of so worthy a

Friend and Fellow alive, as was our Shakespeare' - clearly recalling him with affection. They had worked with him for many years; Shakespeare had left each of them twenty-six shillings and sixpence in his will, to buy a ring to remember him by.

Shakespeare worked with the same company from 1594 until he retired, the longest co-partnership of author and company until that of Gilbert and Sullivan at the end of the nineteenth century. All the time he was working in London, Shakespeare was saving money and investing in property in Stratford, and about 1611 he retired to live in one of the finest houses in the town, New Place. Two years later his old company acted many plays at the celebrations for the marriage of the King's daughter, Princess Elizabeth. Two of them were entitled *The Hotspurre* and *Sir John Falstaffe*, and were probably *Henry IV Parts I* and *II*. About this time Shakespeare wrote at least part of the play *Henry VIII*, probably for this occasion.

Shakespeare died in 1616, and because he was an important and wealthy citizen of the town (where at this time play-acting was banned) he was buried in the chancel of the parish church. A stone with an inscription forbidding the removal of his bones covers his grave, and a stiff, glossy effigy in a niche on the wall looks down on it. But his real memorial is a little way along the river, where in the theatre the Royal Shakespeare Company present his living plays.

1.2 ELIZABETHAN THEATRE

Today if an impresario wishes to put on a play, he can choose any unemployed actors to appear in it, hire a theatre and director, and (if he has enough money) present it. Elizabethan theatre was completely different. There were a number of small companies of men and boys - no women - who travelled around, like the troupe that visits Hamlet's Elsinore. They acted wherever they could collect an audience, in a wide variety of moralities, interludes and plays.

In 1572 a law was passed classing actors with rogues and vagabonds, to be arrested unless they could claim to be servants 'to any Baron of this realm'. So each company had to find a patron, whose 'servants' they nominally were. Shakespeare's company found a patron in Lord Hunsdon, the Queen's cousin, who was Lord Chamberlain. He died in 1596, and they were taken over by his son, as Lord Hunsdon's Men. In 1597 the second Lord Hunsdon became Lord Chamberlain, and the company were once more the Lord Chamberlain's Men. Lastly, when King James I came to the throne in 1603, they must have been the leading company, for only twelve days after he reached London they were appointed to be 'The King's Men'.

They did not only present plays, but were made 'Grooms of the Royal Chamber', who were given scarlet doublets and hose and scarlet cloaks embroidered with the King's cypher in gold; clad thus they attended the King on state occasions.

Since Tudor drama was played by small companies of actors, there had to be doubling of parts. *Cambyses* (to which Falstaff refers at II.iv.394) had 38 characters, but was written so that six men and two boys could play it. In the play *Sir Thomas More* a troupe of four men and a boy offer to perform after dinner. When Sir Thomas says, 'But one boy? Then I see there's but few women in the play', he is told that there are three, and exclaims, 'And one boy play them all? By our Lady, he is overladen.'

London companies grew bigger, but still in 1607 Thomas Heywood's *Fair Maid of the Exchange* had twenty parts, but was arranged so that 'eleven may easily act this comedy'.

Shakespeare had to fit his plays to his company. The Lord Chamberlain's Men contained three groups. First the 'fellows' of the company, whose names were on the royal patent granted to them, which allowed them to act both in London and in provincial cities; they were the 'sharers', who owned the threatre they played in, ran the company, shared the profits, and paid the second group, the 'hired men' for their services. These men acted small parts, took money at the door, prompted, played incidental music, and so on. The third group were the boys, aged between seven and eighteen, apprenticed to senior actors who trained them.

The boys played women's parts until their voices broke – Richard Burbage, the star of the company, complained that the boys 'wore out' too fast. At any one time there would only be two or three boys capable of taking a leading part, hence the shortage of women in Shakespeare's plays. In *Henry IV Part I* there are four big and two other substantial male parts, but only two for women, Mistress Quickly and Lady Percy (who never appear together, so could be doubled) plus the tiny part of Lady Mortimer, who must only be able to sing in Welsh – there must have been a Welsh apprentice at the time. Because Shakespeare fitted his play to the number of actors in the company, it will be found possible to act *Henry IV Part I* with only twelve persons.

Before 1576 the small companies acted anywhere and everywhere, on village greens, or in the halls of colleges or castles or manor houses, or, most often, in the courtyards of inns. But inns, particularly London inns, were busy places where carriers assembled to collect goods for their pack-horses (as we shall see in II.i of *Henry IV Part I*) and the landlords took a large share of the profits. Moreover, the Puritan authorities in the City of London thought play-acting sinful. They objected to the boys acting women's parts, citing *Deuteronomy, xxii.5:* 'The woman shall not wear that which pertaineth to a man, neither shall a man put on a woman's garment, for all that do so are abomination unto the Lord thy God', as a justification for harassing the actors.

So in 1576 James Burbage (father of Richard) built a playhouse in Shoreditch, then a village to the north of the City and outside its jurisdiction. He called it the 'Theatre' - the first English building designed for the presentation of plays. The company which played there was led by Richard Burbage, the greatest actor of the period, and it was this company which Shakespeare joined.

When the lease of the ground on which the Theatre stood expired, the landlord and the Burbages quarrelled. So the actors pulled down the theatre, and ferried its timbers over the Thames to the south side of the river. This was outside the jurisdiction of the City; bull- and bear-baiting rings had been established there, and there were already two theatres, the Rose and the Swan. There in Southwark they built the most famous theatre in the world, the Globe, which Professor Harold Brooks has described at the end of this book.

The public theatres were open to the sky, and a wet summer could be disastrous. In 1608 an indoor theatre, the Blackfriars, became vacant. The impudent company of boy actors who acted satirical pieces there performed a play, *Charles Duke of Byron*, which so offended the French Ambassador that he went off home. King James was annoyed and suppressed the boys' company. The King's Men, with Shakespeare, took over the theatre, and from 1609 had an indoor theatre for winter as well as the Globe for summer performances.

In 1613 a stage cannon fired a red-hot wad into the thatch of the roof of the Globe, and it swiftly burned down. There is no record of the loss of any play-books - when in 1621 the rival theatre, the Fortune, was 'quite burnt down', 'all their apparell and play-books' were lost, and the company ruined. The Burbages rebuilt the Globe, this time with a tiled roof, and it was used until the Puritan Parliament closed all the theatres in 1642.

2 SHAKESPEARE'S ENGLISH HISTORIES

2.1 THE SERIES

Shakespeare's first histories were a series, *Henry VI Parts I, II* and *III* and *Richard III*, covering the years 1422 to 1485, which told the story of the so-called Wars of the Roses, when members of the York and Lancaster families were fighting for the crown. This series ended with the defeat of King Richard III on Bosworth Field by Henry Tudor, who became King Heny VII. But it was not advisable to go on to write the next play about Henry VII, because he was the grandfather of Shakespeare's own Queen, Elizabeth, and too nearly contemporary. It was much safer to avoid current politics on the stage.

So Shakespeare went back to the beginning of the *Chronicles* which he was using for his facts, and composed four plays: *Richard II, Henry IV Parts I* and *II*, and *Henry V*, covering the years 1398 to 1420. An epilogue at the end of *Henry V* points out that this had brought him up to the reign of Henry VI, and so completed the series.

The plays are linked together. The weak King Richard II is deposed by his cousin Henry Bolingbroke, who becomes Henry IV. Richard is murdered, and the Bishop of Carlisle foretells as a result 'woefullest division' (*Richard II*, IV.i.146) and civil war. Richard foresees trouble from Bolingbroke's supporter, Northumberland, and Bolingbroke is worried about the habits of his son Hal, Henry Prince of Wales. All these themes are continued in *Henry IV Parts I* and *II*, which also show the transformation of Hal into the model king, Henry V.

Richard II is written as a conventional tragedy, the fall of an unsatisfactory prince. But in the two parts of *Henry IV* Shakespeare wrote quite a new kind of play. It is a play about political power, but behind the story of rebellion and civil war, king and nobles quarrelling and separating and uniting and fighting and cheating each other, all the time the everyday life of ordinary people is going on, and we get glimpses of it. *Henry IV Part I* is complete in itself; a story of rebellion created and defeated, but (as is usual with Shakespeare) it is told through the lives and characters of individuals. The individuals are not, as in his first series of histories, drawn only from the upper classes, kings and nobles and bishops, but comprise all sorts and conditions of men.

Dr Samuel Johnson, eighteenth-century editor of Shakespeare, said of *Henry IV*, 'Perhaps no author has ever in two plays afforded so much delight', and this delight comes largely from the invented, non-historical figure of the great comic character, Sir John Falstaff (see page 41).

2.2 THE SOURCES

For *Henry IV Part I* Shakespeare's main source was Raphael Holinshed's *Chronicles*. Holinshed had planned a History of the Universe, but the printer who commissioned the work died, and he produced instead the *Chronicles of England, Scotland and Wales*, published in 1578. Shakespeare used the new edition of 1587 (stretching from Noah to contemporary times) not only for his English histories, but also for *Macbeth*, *Cymbeline* and *King Lear*.

From Holinshed's detailed but shapeless narrative the poet Samuel Daniel had already taken material for his long poem, *History of the Civil Wars between the Houses of York and Lancaster*, first published in 1595, and in the third of its four books he gives a clear account of Henry IV's reign. Daniel made one important change: in fact, the rebel Hotspur, Henry Percy, was two years older than King Henry IV, but Daniel, and following him Shakespeare, made Hotspur a generation younger, and the Prince of Wales a little older, so that they could be shown as rivals of about the same age.

Already in *Richard II* Hotspur is addressed as 'boy' and 'young Harry Percy' (II.iii.36, 21), which seems to show that Shakespeare was already planning to make Hotspur into Hal's contemporary. In a later edition Daniel explains that he wrote 'to show the deformities of civil dissension, and the miserable events of rebellions, conspiracies and bloody revengements' which followed Henry IV's deposing of Richard II – and this is precisely Shakespeare's theme in *Henry IV Part I*.

The Elizabethan best-seller, *A Mirror for Magistrates*, telling of the awful fates of wicked rulers, was published in 1559 and enlarged and re-edited six times by 1587. It provided an account of the rebel Owen Glendower. In Holinshed he is a barbarian, but in the *Mirror* a 'crafty dreamer', developed by Shakespeare into a Welsh wizard.

There exists a very corrupt version of a play (or perhaps two plays), *The Famous Victories of Henry V*, just a series of disconnected scenes, which deal with Hal's youthful escapades, and then with his later victories in France, but contain nothing about the rebellions which occupy Shakespeare's *Henry IV*. Shakespeare may well have used the original version of this play for his account of Hal's early wild life. From the *Famous Victories* Shakespeare took only the tale of the Prince's misspent youth, and the name 'Oldcastle' for a disreputable friend of the Prince. Unfortunately, descendants of the real Oldcastle's widow objected very strongly to Sir John Oldcastle's name being given to Shakespeare's fat rogue, so he had to be renamed Falstaff. Is he a 'false staff', no real support to the Prince?

2.3 ELIZABETHAN IDEAS ABOUT HISTORY

Elizabethan historians were not really concerned to produce accurate accounts of what had actually happened in the past, to discover the truth for its own sake, but rather to draw from past events lessons for their own contemporaries. *A Mirror for Magistrates* promised to tell of 'such as are to be followed for their excellency in virtue, or fled for their excellency in vice'. The preface states that 'the goodness or badness of any realm lieth in the goodness or badness of the rulers', and history could teach rulers to be good by showing the tragic downfall of those who were bad. History, it was believed, repeated itself: past events should be studied to throw light on current problems.

The immense and elaborate sixteenth-century tombs in so many English churches, often built before their deaths by the occupants, testify to the Elizabethan desire for 'fame', to be remembered. Queen Elizabeth herself said that her strongest desire was 'to do some act that will make my fame spread abroad in my lifetime, and after, occasion memorial for ever'. It was thought that the knowledge that one's actions would be recorded by historians would inspire men to perform deeds that were worthy and memorable. Shakespeare's Troilus wants to perform 'valiant and magnanimous deeds' so that 'fame in time to come' may 'canonise us' (*Troilus and Cressida*, II.ii.205), and Enobarbus will stick to the disgraced Antony to 'earn a place i' th' story' (*Antony and Cleopatra*, III.iii.46). In *Henry IV Part I* Vernon tells Hotspur that the Prince of Wales 'spoke your deservings like a chronicle' (V.ii.57).

Thomas Heywood, the Elizabethan playwright, trying to persuade the Puritans that plays were good and useful, said that in plays about English heroes, 'so bewitching a thing is lively and well-spirited action that it hath power to new-mould the hearts of the spectators and fashion them to the shape of any noble and notable attempt'. So plays could encourage patriotism.

After the defeat of the Spanish Armada in 1588 there was a surge of nationalistic feeling in England. Medieval Europe had contained the Holy Roman Empire, having one Catholic Church, and a common language, Latin. Now England was on her own, with a Church of England, and with the English language being used even for scholarly books. Shakespeare's English histories, written throughout the 1590s, matched this mood. After beating the Spaniards, people could confidently say with the Bastard Faulconbridge:

> This England never did, nor never shall
> Lie at the proud foot of a conqueror...
> Come the three corners of the world in arms,
> And we shall shock them.   (*King John*, V.vii.112)

We travel England in *Henry IV Part I*. The court is in London, or rather, in Westminster, then a separate city. The tavern is in a particular London street, Eastcheap. Pilgrims to Canterbury and traders and carriers making for Charing Cross (between the Cities of London and Westminster) meet in an inn at Rochester. The River Severn has a sandy bottom and its banks are covered with sedges and reeds, while the 'silver Trent' loops and winds in its course. We hear of the 'Shrewsbury clock', of the goats on the Welsh mountains, and the 'moss-grown towers' in Hotspur's native Northumbria. All are parts of 'this blessed plot, this earth, this realm, this England' (*Richard II*, II.i.50).

Shakespeare took from Holinshed's *Chronicles* the view of history which is called 'the Tudor Myth', because it is history slanted to glorify the Tudors; it is the version which the Tudor monarchs hoped that everyone would believe. It stated that the murder of the anointed King, Richard II, had led to tumult and rebellion for a hundred years, only broken by the short triumphant reign of Henry V. The 'Wars of the Roses' between the Yorkists and the Lancastrians kept the kingdom in turmoil until finally the villainous Richard III was slain by Lancastrian Henry Tudor. He united the contenders by marrying Elizabeth of York, and as Henry VII brought peace and prosperity to England. *Henry IV Part I* begins one year after the murder of Richard II.

3 SUMMARY AND CRITICAL COMMENTARY

3.1 SUMMARY

Henry Bolingbroke of Lancaster has seized the throne from King Richard II, and is now King Henry IV. He is plagued by rebellion in his kingdom and by the bad behaviour of his son Hal, Prince of Wales. The Percy family, the Earls of Northumberland and Worcester, and young Henry Percy (called Hotspur), who placed him on the throne, are now joining with the Welsh Owen Glendower in rebellion. They wish to replace King Henry with Edmund Mortimer, Earl of March, whose father had been named by Richard II as his rightful heir.

Meanwhile the Prince of Wales is idling his time away in the Boar's Head tavern, revelling and play-acting with an aged fat rogue, Sir John Falstaff, and his disreputable companions. The Prince apparently agrees to take part in a highway robbery. In fact, he waits until his companions, including Falstaff, have robbed the travellers, and then robs the thieves, later repaying the stolen money to its owners.

Prince Hal confides to the audience that this is only a temporary holiday, and that in due time he will return to his proper role, as a true prince.

Scenes alternate of the rebels, led by Hotspur, preparing for war, and the Prince fooling in the tavern; but when rebuked by his father the Prince promises to reform, assures the King that he is as good a warrior as Hotspur, and promises to prove this in battle.

Hotspur joins Mortimer (whose sister is Lady Percy, Hotspur's wife) and the Welsh chieftain and wizard, Owen Glendower, in open rebellion. The two armies meet at Shrewsbury. Prince Hal saves the King's life, and defeats Hotspur in single combat. Falstaff, falsely and characteristically, claims credit for Hotspur's death.

The King and Prince are reconciled, and the play ends with the king planning action against further rebellion.

3.2 CRITICAL COMMENTARY

Act I, Scene i

King Henry IV, only one year after he has triumphantly ascended Richard II's throne, seems to be weary, nerve-wracked and prematurely aged. The sad state of the kingdom, England bedaubed with English blood, troubled by 'civil butchery' (13) between 'acquaintance, kindred and allies' (16), is reflected in the sad state of the King, 'So shaken as we are, so wan with care' (1). But as the play begins the King is thinking that for the moment the kingdom is at peace, and that he can lead his nobles on a crusade, thus uniting them in a common purpose, and enabling him to wipe off the sin of Richard's murder. The play *Richard II* ended with Henry's vow:

> I'll make a voyage to the Holy Land
> To wash this blood off from my guilty hand. (V.vi.49)

Now he believes that the opportunity has come. He is immediately disillusioned.

Henry's counsellor and relation by marriage, the Earl of Westmoreland, brings troubling news of fierce fighting in Wales, where the 'irregular and wild Glendower' (40) has slaughtered a thousand of the King's men, led by Edmund Mortimer. Fighting has also broken out in the North, where Hotspur, young Henry Percy (son of the Earl of Northumberland) has defeated the invading Scots and captured 'an honourable spoil, a gallant prize' (74). Westmoreland's tribute – 'it is a conquest for a prince to boast of' (76), merely reminds the King of another and even more severe cause for anxiety.

Young Harry Percy is 'the theme of honour's tongue' (80), but Harry, Prince of Wales, indulges in 'riot and dishonour' (84). The King says he would willingly exchange sons with Lord Northumberland, and the contrast and conflict between the two Harrys is a main theme of the play (see page 72). To make this dramatically effective, Shakespeare made Hotspur and Prince Hal about the same age; historically Hotspur was two or three years older than Hal's father, the King. Yet even Hotspur is not perfect in the King's eyes, for he has only sent one prisoner to the King, and is keeping the ransom for the others himself. Westmoreland, rightly as we shall learn later, suggests that the real villain is Hotspur's uncle, the Earl of Worcester. The scene ends in bustle – Westmoreland must go on the King's business 'with speed'.

Act I, Scene ii

The first scene has been at court, hurried, serious, written in verse, showing messengers and counsellors of the king dealing with matters of state, insurrection and war. It ends with the lean, anxious king hastening to deal with all the problems of the troubled kingdom. Scene ii is slow-moving, frivolous (on the surface at least), written in prose, and opens with a great, gross, idle rogue, Sir John Falstaff, addressing the Prince of Wales with no ceremony at all, 'Now, Hal, what time of day is it, lad?' He gets no precise answer, but a very relevant question: 'What a devil hast thou to do with the time of the day?' (6) For indeed Falstaff takes no heed of time, will stay up all night and sleep all day, since his trade is, he says, 'to take purses', and highway robbers 'go by the moon and the seven stars' and not by 'Phoebus', the sun. ('Go by' implies both 'tell the time by' and 'go out by the light of'.)

Falstaff seems to have all the time in the world just to laze and jest; it is as if he is merely passing the time till the moment arrives which he repeatedly invokes while talking to the Prince: 'when thou art king' (16, 23, 63, 65, 152). He continually emphasises Hal's rank, 'sweet young prince', 'king's son', 'the blood royal', 'true prince' (85, 103, 146, 160); but never treats him with the respect due, in Elizabethan eyes, to royalty.

Falstaff's speech is full of puns, words which can be understood in more than one way. He romanticises robbery, but the Prince is realistic about its outcome, the gallows (see pages 55 and 65).

Falstaff tries to change this uncomfortable subject but then uneasily returns to it, as he will many times during the play, 'Shall there be gallows standing in England when thou art king? And resolution thus fubbed as it is with the rusty curb of old father antic the law? Do not thou, when thou art king, hang a thief' (62). Shall courage be robbed of its due reward by that old ridiculous creature, the law? Here Falstaff exhibits his true irresponsibility as a lawless anarchist, and the Prince responds briefly: 'No, thou shalt' (67). Falstaff ignores the possibly sinister meaning (thou shalt hang), and takes it as a compliment: 'I'll be a brave judge!' (69), he cries, only to be cruelly put down by Hal: 'I mean, thou shalt. . .become a rare hangman'. To the Elizabethans the hangman seemed a necessary part of the state, but a very low one. Falstaff is temporarily embarrassed, and for once at a loss for immediate response: 'Well, Hal, well. . .'. But, as ever, he soon recovers his poise, and jokes about the hangman's wardrobe – the clothes of those he hanged were the hangman's 'perks'.

Talk of hanging changes Falstaff's mood. With assumed piety he starts to pay lip-service to the good life, and to parody the sanctimonious style of the Puritans. Reversing the real state of affairs, he rebukes the Prince for leading him into evil ways: 'trouble me no more with vanity' (86); 'thou. . .art indeed able to corrupt a saint' (96).

Throughout the play Falstaff will indulge frequently in mock repentance: 'I must give over this life, and I will give it over' (101). But as soon as Hal tests him by proposing to 'take a purse', Falstaff brightens, and responds, 'Where thou wilt, lad. I'll make one'. When the Prince teases him, 'I see a good amendment of life in thee - from praying to purse-taking' (108), Falstaff has a witty answer ready: 'Tis my vocation, Hal. 'Tis no sin for a man to labour in his vocation.'

Again Falstaff turns to his own purposes a popular Puritain text (*I Corinthians*, vii.20) which was echoed in the *Homily against Idleness*: so every one. . .ought. . .to exercise himself according to the vocation where unto God hath called him'. Since the *Homilies* were regularly read in church as sermons, and weekly churchgoing was compulsory, the audience in the Elizabethan theatre would appreciate Falstaff's continual parodies much more than any twentieth-century audience can.

When the Prince's companion Poins enters, hailing Falstaff as 'Monsieur Remorse' (118), we realise that this is not the first time that Falstaff has briefly 'repented'.

Poins has discovered that at Gadshill in Kent there are rich pilgrims going to Canterbury and rich traders travelling to London, and proposes to waylay them. (Shakespeare for once is picturing medieval rather than Elizabethan England; there were no Elizabethan pilgrimages - at least none undertaken openly.) Falstaff invites Hal to join the gang, but he replies, apparently astonished, 'Who, I rob? I a thief? Not I by my faith' (144); but being pressed says '*once* in my days I'll be a madcap' (148), as if he had never before joined in such an escapade. Changing his mind he goes on, 'I'll tarry at home' (150). Falstaff threatens: 'I'll be a traitor then, when thou art king' (151) and ignores the ominous note in the Prince's brief reply: 'I care not'.

Shakespeare is ambiguous, as so often, and it is the reader who, remembering the Prince's inclusion of himself in 'the moon's men' (32), must decide whether or not the Prince had actually been a highwayman before.

Poins persuades the Prince to accompany them; not to take part in the hold-up and actual robbery, but to wait until Falstaff and company have waylaid the travellers, and then rob the thieves. Later at supper, they will all be amused by Falstaff's 'incomprehensible lies' (191) when he tries to explain the failure of the expedition.

It is noticeable in this scene that Falstaff speaks to the Prince disrespectfully, but with real affection: 'sweet wag', 'lad', 'mad wag', 'sweet young prince', but the Prince never uses a similar tone, and administers several severe snubs.

Left by himself, the Prince then speaks a soliloquy, a speech made when alone on the stage, and in the Elizabethan theatre spoken directly to the audience (who, it must be remembered, were clearly visible to the actors in the unroofed theatre). This speech makes it clear that when Hal said to Falstaff, 'I care not' (153) this was literally true, and that he feels no obligation to his tavern acquaintances. After the quick backchat with

Poins and Falstaff, the formal verse of this soliloquy strikes coldly on the ear, and emphasises the complete change of mood.

The Prince declares that it is only for a short time, 'awhile', that he will live 'unyoked' in this world of idleness, that is, not harnessed to do a useful job. Far from being one of the 'moon's men', he compares himself to the emblem of kingship, the sun, and his companions to the 'base contagious clouds' that temporarily hide its glory - 'contagious' is a strong word implying that the clouds bring disease, especially plague. Hal emphasises that his tavern persona is false by saying that he will change 'to be himself', the true prince.

Tavern life is 'playing holidays' and indefinite holidays grow boring. In any case, how much more conspicuous and admired his transformation to good behaviour will be, when no one expects it from such a dissolute youth.

If this speech is regarded as a true personal expression of Hal's thoughts and feelings, it makes him seem a disagreeable hypocrite. But it is possible to understand it as conveying, like a chorus, information to the audience. It lets them know that this prince, despite appearances, is not the rowdy wastrel shown in the play *The Famous Victories of Henry V*, nor even the debauched 'young wanton and effeminate boy. . .as dissolute as desperate' lamented by his father in Shakespeare's preceding play *Richard II* (V.iii.10, 20).

Dr Johnson, the great eighteenth-century editor of Shakespeare, thought that the speech's function was 'to keep the Prince from appearing vile in the opinion of the audience'. But if the Prince is really saying that he is only sporting with Falstaff as a publicity stunt, so that when he reforms people will be amazed and delighted, then he does appear a 'vile' humbug. Or is he making up reasons to excuse a way of life which he truly enjoys? Or is he (as the Earl of Warwick suggests in *Henry IV Part II*) deliberately trying to acquaint himself with all sorts and conditions of men, over whom he will one day have to rule?

At least it can be agreed that this speech shows the Prince as a thoughtful and serious character, and not the lightweight which the King (and Hotspur) imagine him to be. It is now clear that this play tells neither the traditional story of the prodigal son, nor that of the dissolute young prince who reforms and is converted from evil to goodness. Hal is not dissolute. He is a prince, and one day, inescapably, he will be a king, with all the burdens which his father finds so heavy. Hal is, while he may, 'playing holiday'.

A king cannot disregard time; soon Hal must indeed know precisely the time of day, and he ends his speech by promising to redeem time, that is, to use it to the best advantage:

> I'll so offend to make offence a skill,
> Redeeming time when men think least I will. (221)

And when at last he does become Henry V, Shakespeare tells us later that he 'weighs time even to the utmost grain' (*Henry V*, II.iv.138).

In this scene we have been shown two very different aspects of the Prince: the playboy and the dutiful heir to the throne.

Act I, Scene iii

Now we find rebellion growing, and are given a full picture of Hal's rival, Hotspur. From the Prince in the tavern, cold-bloodedly summing-up his plans, we move to the court, where we find his father, King Henry, testifying that his blood has been 'too cold and temperate' in overlooking the independent behaviour of the Percy family.

The relation between the King and the Percys was bound to be uneasy. When King Henry's father, John of Gaunt, died, King Richard II seized all his lands, which Henry should have inherited. The Percys, with other nobles who feared that their lands too would be seized from their heirs, deposed Richard, and Henry Bolingbroke succeeded as King Henry IV. Henry fears that, not feeling sufficiently rewarded for what they have done, the Percys may try to depose him. They know that the king does not trust them, and bitterly resent his elevation over them.

Worcester dares to point out that Henry is not King by natural succession, but owes his throne to their support, and is immediately dismissed by the angry King. His brother, Northumberland, assures the King that his son, Hotspur, has been misreported; he had not refused to send his prisoners to the King. Hotspur tries to justify himself in a fiery speech.

Hotspur paints a vivid picture of the battlefield, and his own exhaustion – 'dry with rage and extreme toil' (30). When a mincing, effeminate courtier, who had taken no part in the fighting, came to him chattering, taking snuff, objecting to the smell of corpses, and demanding the prisoners in the king's name, Hotspur could not bear to be 'so pestered with a popinjay' (49), and answered at random. Full of life and fire, heated but enough in control to mimic the courtier and make fun of him, with his 'holiday and lady terms' (45) and his declaration that 'but for these vile guns, He would himself have been a soldier' (62), Hotspur seems very much the princely warrior whom Henry would like to have for a son.

The King's wise and faithful counsellor, Sir Walter Blunt, begs the King to forget the report of Hotspur's words 'to such a person and in such a place' (71), but the King is adamant. Hotspur asks the King to ransom his brother-in-law Mortimer, captured by Glendower. (Shakespeare treats as one man the two historical Mortimers: one was Sir Edmund, who married Glendower's daughter, the other his nephew, the Earl of March, who had a substantial claim to the throne, as Richard II had named his father as heir to the crown.) Naturally King Henry IV is delighted to have a claimant to the throne imprisoned in Wales: 'on the barren mountains let him starve!' (88). The King will never ransom 'revolted Mortimer', but Hotspur rashly continues to demand Mortimer's rescue, describing his tremendous hand-to-hand struggle with Glendower. The King lets fly in royal rage a parting command:

> Let me not hear you speak of Mortimer. . .
> Send us your prisoners, or you will hear of it. (117, 122)

Hotspur explodes with rage; his father and his uncle Worcester do their best to calm him, but in vain. Worcester enrages Hotspur further by saying that the deposed Richard had named Mortimer as his heir. Hotspur declares that it is bad enough that his father and uncle put down 'Richard, that sweet lovely rose' (173) in favour of 'this canker, Bolingbroke' (174) but worse still now that the ungrateful King is casting them off. As Hotspur urges revenge, Worcester interrupts, promising to tell him

> matter deep and dangerous,
> As full of peril and adventurous spirit
> As to o'erwalk a current roaring loud
> On the unsteadfast footing of a spear. (188)

This vividly pictured ordeal is just the kind of exploit to appeal to Hotspur, but he is too excited to let Worcester tell him about the plan, whatever it is. Hotspur welcomes danger, so long as it brings 'honour'. There will be much talk of 'honour' in this play. To Hotspur it means military prowess, fame in the eyes of his peers. Danger is nothing; he will leap to the moon or dive to the ocean bed if only he ends with 'honour'.

Hotspur has lost control of himself; Worcester tries to speak but is continually interrupted. The difference in the movement of the blank verse between Worcester's measured speech and Hotspur's impulsive exclamations, breaking up the lines of verse, shows how Shakespeare varies speech rhythms according to situation and character.

> WORCESTER He apprehends a world of figures here,
> But not the form of what he should attend.
> Good cousin give me audience for a while.
> HOTSPUR I cry you mercy.
> WORCESTER Those same noble Scots
> That are your prisoners –
> HOTSPUR I'll keep them all!
> By God, he shall not have a Scot of them!
> No, if a Scot would save his soul, he shall not.
> I'll keep them, by this hand.

> WORCESTER   You start away
> And lend no ear unto my purposes.
> These prisoners you shall keep –
> HOTSPUR   Nay, I will! That's flat! (207)

When Hotspur remembers that he was told never to speak of Mortimer, he bursts our childishly:

> . . .I'll have a starling shall be taught to speak
> Nothing but 'Mortimer', and give it him
> To keep his anger still in motion. (233)

Scorning the Prince of Wales for his tavern life, Hotspur would have him poisoned with 'a pot of ale' (not a drink for a proper prince) – if it were not that that, he thinks, might please the King. His wily uncle and father are disgusted by Hotspur's lack of control, but cannot stop him until he has recalled his first meeting with Bolingbroke who, returning from exile and needing the help of the Percys, treated Hotspur then with 'fawning' courtesy (248), so unlike his present regal attitude.

Committed to treason, Worcester dispatches Hotspur to foment trouble in Scotland, and Northumberland to 'creep into the bosom' of the disaffected Archbishop of York, Scroop, while he himself will 'steal' to Glendower and Mortimer. 'Creep' and 'steal' suggest the underhand nature of their plotting.

Without a moment's consideration, Hotspur immediately declares that the conspiracy 'will do well' (271), and is 'a noble plot' (274). Recklessly he welcomes war as a game:

> O let the hours be short
> Till fields and blows and groans applaud our sport! (296)

Hotspur's fierce nature and rash impulsiveness are the greatest possible contrast to the foreseeing, calculating Prince Hal of the scene before.

Act II, Scene i

Since Shakespeare's theatre had neither changeable lighting nor painted scenery, he had to indicate the time and place of a scene through the actors. Now two carriers enter with a lantern (showing that it is dark), yawning and telling by the stars that it is four o'clock in the morning, calling to the ostler to fetch their horses. Their speech is absolutely naturalistic: 'This house is turned upside down since Robin Ostler died.' 'Poor fellow never joyed since the price of oats rose; it was the death of him.' (II.i.10). We learn that one has bacon and ginger, and the other young turkeys, to be delivered at Charing Cross, and these touches of detail seem to establish the reality of the scene.

They draw a very unsavoury picture of an Elizabethan inn, damp, stinking of urine, full of fleas, and what's more, inhabited by a chamberlain (an inn servant) in league with highwaymen, who reports the arrival of any rich travellers to Falstaff's ally, Gadshill.

Highway robbers were known as 'St Nicholas' clerks', and if caught soon wore the 'necklace' or noose of the hangman. But Gadshill brushes aside the danger. He hints that some of his gangs are not poor robbers, but have joined 'for sport sake' (71) and are powerful enough to hush up any trouble.

Act II, Scene ii

On the highway, the Prince and Poins have removed Falstaff's horse, and he enters breathless and panting, but continually complaining. As an example of Shakespeare's use of the conditions of his theatre, Poins should be at the front of the great stage, where the Prince joins him, hiding from Falstaff behind a pillar. Falstaff enters from the opposite corner, having then a long walk diagonally, giving him a superb opportunity to puff and pant during his speech. Even when talking to himself, Falstaff makes jokes and shrewd comments; 'A plague upon it,' he says, 'when thieves cannot be true one to another' (27) and we are reminded that we have just seen the noble thieves who stole King Richard's throne falling out, and that the Prince and Poins are conspiring to cheat Falstaff.

Falstaff's bulk is never forgotten. The Prince tells 'fat-guts' (31) to lie down and listen for the tread of travellers, but Falstaff immediately enquires, 'Have you any levers to lift me up again, being down?' (34) None of them will help Falstaff to his horse, and when Gadshill appears and cries 'Stand!' (49) Falstaff ruefully answers (when he has recovered from his fright) 'So I do against my will' (50).

When Gadshill talks of the travellers' wealth – 'There's enough to make us all. . .' (58) Falstaff interrupts, and instead of some cheerful prospect such as 'rich for life', says 'to be hanged' (59) – an apprehension of his likely fate never far from his mind.

All proceeds according to Poins' plan; Falstaff and his gang rob the travellers, and while the loot is being shared out, the Prince and Poins set upon them and steal the money. Even Falstaff, 'after a blow or two' waddles away, and the Prince unkindly observes that 'he sweats to death, and lards the lean earth as he walks along' (111) – the Elizabethans believed that sweat consisted of liquid fat.

Act II, Scene iii

While Hal is joining in a fight as a practical joke, Hotspur plans to fight in earnest. Rebellion was a deadly sin, and some of the Percys' allies are getting cold feet, and withdrawing from the conspiracy. Hotspur has a letter from one of them, and comments fiercely and bitterly on its contents.

The faithless writer puts forward sober arguments – Hotspur's purpose is dangerous, his allies uncertain, the timing ill-chosen, the King too powerful. Hotspur's only answer is bluster: 'our plot is a good plot as ever was laid; our friends true and constant; a good plot, good friends, and full of expectation; an excellent plot, very good friends' (16). The writer may be a 'shallow cowardly hind' (15); Hotspur seems a very reckless lion, though he admits alarm lest this 'pagan rascal' (29) should warn the King of their plotting.

Hotspur may appear confident. His worried wife tells a different story. Loneliness, and seeking solitude, were to the Elizabethans symptoms of ill-health, of melancholy. Rooms led into each other, and life was lived very much in public, in groups. Only villains like Richard III would say 'I am myself alone' (*Henry VI Part III*, V.vi.83), or like Iago, 'I follow but myself' (*Othello*, I.i.58). Lady Percy (called 'Kate' by Shakespeare) has seen Hotspur's solitary wanderings, and heard him muttering, in his restless sleep 'tales of iron wars' (49). She begs him to confide in her, but Hotspur ignores her and calls for his roan horse. When, in real distress, she implores him to say 'what is it carries you away?' (76), he simply replies, 'Why, my horse, my love, my horse!' (77)

Her anxious, loving enquiries are evaded; Hotspur keeps love and war apart:

> This is no world
> To play with mammets and to tilt with lips.
> We must have bloody noses and cracked crowns. (92)

Some critics have found in this scene evidence of a close love-relationship between Hotspur and Kate; others have seen in Hotspur's

> Away, you trifler! Love? I love thee not;
> I care not for thee, Kate, (91)

followed by her desperate

> Do you not love me? Do you not, indeed?...
> Nay, tell me if you speak in jest or no, (97)

less evidence of this. But after refusing to trust her with his secrets, Hotspur does tell her that their parting will be short – 'Whither I go, thither shall you go too' (116), and with that she has to be content.

Act II, Scene iv

In the tavern the Prince has, he says, 'sounded the very base [bass] string of humility' (5) by drinking with the pot-boys; he has won their affection, and perhaps his education is continuing as he learns to 'drink with any tinker in his own language' (19). But there follows a scene which today seems distasteful, when Poins and the Prince combine to tease and confuse a slow-witted young apprentice, Francis.

Then 'I am of all humours' (90) says Hal, and proceeds to try another role. He parodies Hotspur, as we have seen him in the preceding scene, killing 'some six or seven dozen of Scots' (104) then saying to his wife, 'Fie upon this quiet life! I want work' (106), and neglecting to answer his wife while thinking of his 'roan horse' (108). The Prince mocks Hotspur's heroics, as later he mocks Falstaff's exaggerated praise of the Douglas (338-50).

This play-acting calls for more – Hal says he will be Percy, and 'that damned brawn', Falstaff, will play Dame Mortimer, his wife. But a different play is enacted, as Falstaff enters, grumbling in his mock-Puritan way, and lamenting the state of the world.

The robbery has failed, and Falstaff is determined not to accept the blame. 'A plague of all cowards, I say' he repeats (115, 118, 135, 158, 173), accusing the Prince and Poins of deserting him. He delivers a highly inaccurate account of the expedition, of his own bravery, and how he beat off 'two rogues in buckram suits' (196). 'Four rogues in buckram let drive at me', he goes on, and the four become seven, nine, eleven, plus three more 'knaves in Kendal green' (225), in an uproarious charade. 'These lies,' says Hal, 'are like their father that begat them – gross as a mountain, open palpable' (229), and he gives a plain, simple account of what actually happened, how he and Poins alone drove the gang from their prize, and how Falstaff had 'run and roared' (265).

All seems lost. How can Falstaff explain or recover? Quick-wittedly he replies, 'I knew ye as well as he that made ye. . .was it for me to kill the heir apparent?. . .beware instinct. The lion will not touch the true prince. . . .I was a coward on instinct' (273). (When the Prince's great-grandfather, Edward III, was disputing with Philip V, each claiming to be the true King of France, it was seriously proposed that both monarchs should enter a lion's den, and the one that was not eaten would clearly be the true prince.)

Cheered by the thought of the booty in the Prince's keeping, Falstaff echoes the Prince's proposal that they should have 'a play extempore' (286). Then news comes of the Percys' rebellion, the Prince is summoned to court next morning. Now Shakespeare inserts – as he often did – a play within the play, when the Prince and Falstaff assume, and then exchange, parts. Falstaff suggests that Hal will be 'horribly chid' by his father, and that they should rehearse the interview; clapping a cushion on his head for a crown, Falstaff prepares to act the part of King Henry.

This scene is extremely complicated. Falstaff, who longs to be a father-figure to his 'sweet young prince', acts the king 'in King Cambyses vein' (394). 'King Cambyses' was a ranting part for Edward Alleyn, leading actor in a rival company to Shakespeare's, so presumably the actor playing Falstaff now adopted some of Alleyn's mannerisms. The hostess may well have had Alleyn in mind when she says, 'He doth it as like one of these harlotry players as ever I see' (404).

Falstaff, as King Henry, mockingly scolds the Prince, but slips in one significant question. Can it really be right for 'the son [sun] of England [to] prove a thief and take purses?' (418) And then, speaking for himself rather than as the King, he goes on to advise the Prince to stick to a 'virtuous man. . .a goodly portly man,. . .his name is Falstaff. . .there is virtue in that Falstaff. Him keep with, the rest banish' (428). Having made his plea, Falstaff resorts to frivolity, and the Prince cannot bear to hear his father so mocked any longer: 'Do thou stand for me and I'll play my father.' (442)

They change places and roles, and the Prince, speaking as the King, pours out revolting physical descriptions of Falstaff, the 'devil' who haunts his son, 'that villainous abominable misleader of youth' (472). The vehemence and seriousness of the attack alarm Falstaff, and he slips out of his part as the Prince to defend himself with sincerity and eloquence.

'If to be fat be to be hated, then Pharoah's lean kine are to be loved. No, my good lord; banish Peto, banish Bardolph, banish Poins; but for sweet Jack Falstaff, kind Jack Flastaff, true Jack Falstaff, valiant Jack Falstaff, and therefore more valiant being, as he is, old Jack Falstaff, banish not him thy Harry's company, banish not him thy Harry's company, banish plump Jack, and banish all the world!' (482) Unmoved, the Prince, speaking as his father, as himself, and as the king he will become, answers uncompromisingly, 'I do, I will.' (491) He thus repeats to Falstaff's face the resolution which we heard him make when alone; he will discard these companions, including Falstaff, as soon as it suits him, when the political situation makes it necessary.

Falstaff can't, or won't, believe what he hears; but the tension is broken by bustle when the sheriff arives with the watch, and Falstaff's thoughts at once turn to hanging. But the Prince tells him to hide, and promises the sheriff to make all well. Falstaff, clearly relying absolutely on the Prince to save him, is found snoring behind the curtains, and the Prince lets him sleep on.

But the mood has changed. The shadow of the court has fallen on the tavern. Hal has responsibilities which he must recognise: 'We must all to the wars' (556), he says, and 'The [stolen] money shall be paid back again with advantage' (559). (The *Chronicles* have a story of Hal robbing his own tax gatherers, and then giving the money back, with rewards to those who had resisted bravely.)

Act III, Scene i

The rebels meet in Wales. Owen Glendower is pictured in Holinshed's *Chronicles* as a fierce warrier 'robbing and spoiling within the English borders', whose army mutilated the corpses of his fallen enemies, and who 'through art magike' caused 'such foul weather' that the king's army had to withdraw. Shakespeare shows him at home, warrior, poet and musician, with some slight magical power and a strong belief in astrology.

Glendower and his son-in-law Mortimer are meeting Hotspur and his uncle, the Earl of Worcester, to finalise their plans. Glendower boasts that there were earthquakes and fiery portents in the sky at his birth (striking, but far less awesome than the account in Holinshed: 'all his father's horses in the stable were found to stand in blood up to the bellies'.) Sceptical Hotspur rudely claims that the earthquakes were caused by the earth's indigestion, and 'unruly wind within her womb' breaking out, as both ancient Greeks and Elizabethans believed. He says the same portents would have occurred 'if your mother's cat had but kittened' (17).

Glendower and Hotspur bicker on till Glendower claims, 'I can call spirits from the vasty deep' (52), and Hotspur answers like a cheeky schoolboy:

> Why, so can I, or so can any man;
> But will they come when you do call for them? (53)

Glendower produces a map, and they proceed to divide England into three separate parts. This alone would damn them in Elizabethan eyes, for the Tudors' claim to respect rested largely on the belief that they had united an England split by civil war.

All seems agreed until Hotspur (who at first was so indifferent to material gain that he had 'forgot the map' (5)) suddenly decides that his share is too small, and there is an outburst of childish wrangling. Hotspur recklessly ridicules Glendower, and the Welsh language, and Glendower's ability to write 'mincing poetry' (132). Glendower controls himself and offers Hotspur the desired land, only to have it thrust back. Hotspur says he will be generous to a friend:

> But in the way of bargain, mark ye me,
> I'll cavil on the ninth part of a hair. (136)

When Glendower retires, Hotspur expresses a violent distaste for his talk and personality. Mortimer entreats Hotspur to stop provoking Glendower, who seems to his son-in-law to be 'worthy', 'exceedingly well-read', 'affable' and 'bountiful', and who has been, as we have seen, extraordinarily forbearing to a rude guest. Worcester, too, realising that Hotspur's behaviour will be fatal to the success of the rebellion, condemns him for his

> Defect of manners, want of government,
> Pride, haughtiness, opinion and disdain (181),

all of them qualities disgraceful in a nobleman. These things lose men's hearts, and, as Worcester and Hal appreciate, and Hotspur does not, a leader must be popular, or at least liked by his colleagues and followers. Hotspur rather sulkily accepts their 'schooling', hoping cynically that their good manners will bring them good fortune on the battlefield.

The atmosphere changes as the Ladies Percy and Mortimer come to bid farewell to their hubands. Mortimer and Glendower's daughter are in love, but can only communicate by embraces ('My wife can speak no English, I no Welsh', but 'I understand thy kisses, and thou mine' (191, 203).) Mortimer lies down and rests his head in his wife's lap, while she sings a Welsh song, accompanied by magic music played by spirits, who do come when Glendower calls them.

Now, as so often in Shakespeare, we are shown a relationship which actors can interpret in various ways, that between Hotspur and Kate. She is, as before, devoted, but he, as before, is fretting to be gone. His words are deliberately coarse: 'Come, Kate, thou art perfect in lying down' (231) – as he imitates, or in fact parodies, the other romantic (or sentimental?) pair. He continues brash; he would prefer his dog's howling to Welsh music, and when his wife refuses to sing, 'in good sooth' [in truth] he rebukes her for her feeble bourgeois restraint, and begs her to swear aristocratically, 'a good mouth-filling oath' (254). But all the time 'hot Lord Percy is on fire to go' (264) to the real business of his life – battle.

We will see that Hotspur uses love words only when describing war; his horse will bear him, he says, 'against the bosom of the Prince of Wales' (IV.i.121); 'I will embrace him with a soldier's arm' (V.ii.73); and he bids his allies 'all embrace' before the battle (V.ii.98).

Act III, Scene ii

From the uneasy alliance of the rebels in Wales we come back to an uneasy relationship in London. This is the interview rehearsed in the tavern. King Henry has sent for the Prince, and bitterly blames him for his low way of life. It is clear that the King is deeply grieved and angered by this disgraceful public spectacle; how much is he saddened by their personal estrangement?

Henry describes how carefully, before he was King, he created the right image of himself, appearing rarely, but always modestly courteous to everyone. This recalls King Richard's resentment when Henry (still Bolingbroke) 'did seem to dive into [the people's] hearts, with humble and familiar courtesy' (*Richard II*, I.iv.25). We now learn that this was part of a deliberate scheme to create an image far different from that of

Richard, 'the skipping king' who 'mingled his royalty with capering fools' (60, 63).

Prince Hal is overwhelmed by the King's passion and grief. He does not promise to change, but to 'be more myself' (92), implying as he did before that his present persona is temporary and assumed.

When King Henry goes on to praise Hotspur's 'never-dying honour', calling him 'Mars in swaddling clothes' (106, 112), and even suggesting that Hal will 'fight against me under Percy's pay' (126), Hal responds with real passion: 'Do not think so; you shall not find it so' (129). The Prince bitterly recognises the difference in public estimation between 'this gallant Hotspur, this all-praisèd knight' and 'your unthought-of Harry' (140). He swears that one day he will fight with Hotspur, and make him 'render every glory up' (150). Hal pleads so eloquently that the King appoints him to a command in the army marching against the rebels, who have met at Shrewsbury. We leave the King organising his forces, and return to the tavern for the last time.

Act III, Scene iii

Immense and rubicund, Falstaff enters complaining that he has 'fallen away', dwindled, 'withered', 'my skin hangs about me like an old lady's loose gown. . .Well, I'll repent. . .while I am *in some liking*. I shall be *out of heart* shortly, and then I shall have no strength to repent' (1). 'In some liking' means 'plump' and 'out of heart' means 'in a poor state of health'. Perhaps Falstaff is unconsciously prophesying that through the Prince likes him at the moment, he may soon be out of the Prince's heart. But a moment later he is calling for a bawdy song, and comically recalling his life of dicing, lechery and debt. Will the repentance of the Prince be equally short-lived?

Falstaff turns on the Hostess, claiming that his pocket was picked of valuables; but we know that when Poins searched him (II.iv.544) Falstaff's pocket contained nothing but bills. Falstaff uses his wit to confuse and baffle the Hostess, and is threatening that he will cudgel the Prince, when suddenly Hal appears, marching in with Peto, as if soldiers. Falstaff immediately pretends that the truncheon which he is waving threateningly is a fife, and pretends to play a tune on it.

The hostess appeals to the Prince, while Falstaff tries to shout her down, and though their exchanges can be very comic, as when Falstaff eggs her on to declare her availability to any man (134), in sober fact Falstaff is trying to cheat a woman who has looked after him generously. In the end Falstaff is impudent enough to 'forgive' her the wrongs which he has done to her (177).

There is one exchange of real significance, when the Prince challenges Falstaff, 'Sirrah, do I owe you a thousand pounds?' and is answered with desperate sincerity and longing, 'A thousand pounds, Hal? A million! Thy love is worth a million, thou owest me thy love' (140).

The Prince assures Falstaff that the robbery has been hushed up, and the stolen money paid back, but when Falstaff suggests that the reconciliation with the King will enable the Prince to rob the Exchequer, he is ignored. For the Prince is not here today to fool about. He tells Falstaff (as he threatened before) that Falstaff will have an infantry command, involving marching, and must come the next day for orders, tells Bardolph to deliver letters to other commanders, and exits on a Hotspur-like couplet:

> The land is burning, Percy stands on high,
> And either we or they must lower lie. (209)

Although there is much comedy in this scene, Falstaff is becoming a less appealing character, witty as ever, but it may be true that he has 'more flesh than another man and therefore more frailty' (173); 'there's no room for faith, truth nor honesty in this bosom of thine. It is all filled up with guts and midriff' (158).

Act IV, Scene i
In the rebel camp things are not going well. Hotspur's father, Northumberland, fails them. Instead of bringing, or even sending, his forces, he sends letters to say that he is sick, but that they must press on without him. It is too late to withdraw, since by now the King must know all their plans.

Hotspur, and the equally rash Douglas, feel (like Henry V before Agincourt) 'the fewer men the greater share of honour' (*Henry V*, IV.iii.22). But the politic Worcester is realistic about this blow; not only is their army reduced, but their morale; people will think that 'wisdom, loyalty and mere [absolute] dislike of [their] proceedings' kept Northumberland at home, or even perhaps 'a kind of fear' (64, 74). Fiery, irrational Hotspur gives evidence of his unsuitability for rule when he proposes to 'o'erturn [the kingdom] topsy-turvey down' (82) and insists that 'yet all goes well' (83); Douglas boasts that in Scotland the word 'fear' is never spoken.

Vernon brings news of the approach of Westmoreland and Prince John with seven thousand men, and the King too, with 'strong and mighty preparation' (93). Hotspur brushes this aside, but asks where is the 'nimble-footed madcap Prince of Wales' (95). To his amazement Vernon utters a paean of praise of the Prince and his companions (see page 59). The astounded Hotspur can only threaten:

> Harry to Harry shall, hot horse to horse,
> Meet, and ne'er part till one drop down a corse. (122)

Vernon reports that Glendower will not come for fourteen days, and though this was arranged in Wales (III.i.83) Douglas and Worcester are chilled by the 'frosty' news, and even Hotspur can only sound defiant: 'Doomsday is near. Die all, die merrily' (134).

To fight will now be a rash gamble. Later, rebels recalling the battle will say that Hotspur

> 'with great imagination
> Proper to madmen, led his powers to death,
> And, winking [with closed eyes], leaped into destruction.'
> (*Henry IV Part II*, I.iii.31)

Act IV, Scene ii

Everyone is now moving towards Shrewsbury. Armed with the King's warrant, Falstaff has recruited a company of soldiers. But what soldiers! He has conscripted good solid men, householders, bridegrooms, men unwilling to leave home or to fight, and they have bribed him to let them stay at home. He is left with a miserable ragged crew; he compares them to scarecrows, to the tattered prodigal son who was reduced to eating the husks given to the swine he tended, and to the corpses that hung decaying from gibbets. They are useless as soldiers: 'such toasts-and-butter, with hearts in their bellies no bigger than pins' heads' (21).

The Prince calls them 'pitiful rascals' (65), but pity is not one of Falstaff's emotions. To him they are 'food for powder' who will 'fill a pit as well as better' (66): when they are dead he will continue to draw and pocket their pay. Westmoreland complains that they are 'exceedingly poor and bare, too beggarly' (70); Falstaff declares that 'for their bareness. . . they never learnt that of me' (72), as usual turning aside criticism by jests about his own bulk. When urged to hasten to the battlefield Falstaff sums himself up: 'To the latter end of a fray and the beginning of a feast fits a dull [unenthusiastic] fighter and a keen guest' (80).

Act IV, Scene iii

The rebels are still quarrelling. Hotspur and Douglas, headstrong and eager, are anxious to join battle at once; Vernon and Worcester wish to wait till the next morning. Douglas accuses Vernon of 'fear and cold heart' (7), and he retorts hotly, but also produces good reasons for delay.

They are interrupted by Sir Walter Blunt, an envoy from King Henry. He courteously asks the rebels to name their grievances, and promises to redress these, and to pardon all who have risen against him, 'misled' by the Percys' 'suggestions' – 'suggestion' as used by Shakespeare has implications that what is 'suggested' is evil.

Hotspur answers satirically. He pours out his version of Bolingbroke's return from exile, 'a poor unminded outlaw sneaking home' (58), who swore that he came only for his rightful inheritance, which had been seized by King Richard, and was supported and befriended by the kind Northumberland. In fact, Northumberland and the other nobles joined Bolingbroke in order to stop Richard seizing their lands also. And while Bolingbroke was still sending messages of 'allegiance and true faith of heart' to King Richard, Northumberland had already dropped the title, referred to the King as 'Richard', and had been rebuked for it by the Duke of York (*Richard II*, III.iii.37, 6-9). But, says Hotspur, Bolingbroke went further, cut off the heads of Richard's favourites, deposed the King and had him murdered, and refused to ransom Mortimer.

Then comes a personal grievance; King Henry, Hotspur says, 'disgraced me in my happy victories' (97) (that is, he demanded my prisoners), spied on him, dismissed his father and uncle, 'broke oath on oath' (101) – so that rebellion was the only solution.

Despite all this, the conciliatory Blunt begs them to accept the King's 'grace and love' (112); Hotspur, surprisingly, says 'And may be so we shall' (113), and the parley is adjourned.

Act IV, Scene iv

In this short scene the Archbishop of York is sending 'suggestions' of further rebellion far and wide, showing us that even if the King wins at Shrewsbury, his troubles will be far from over.

The Archbishop is worried; the King has a 'mighty. . .power [army]' (12); Northumberland's forces have not appeared; Glendower has been 'o'er-ruled by prophecies' (18) and neither he nor Mortimer are with the rebel forces. The Archbishop fears that if King Henry beats the Percys, he will certainly try to root out the Archbishop's confederates before disbanding his army.

This scene is very often cut in performance, and indeed its only use is to prepare listeners for the action in *Henry IV Part II*, which is also foreshadowed at the very end of *Part I*.

Act V, Scene i

Nature seems ominous next morning. The sun rises 'bloodily', the daylight is 'pale' and the wind like a trumpet summons them to the 'tempest' of battle. Worcester and Vernon come to parley with the King who (talking like an old, worn-out man) rebukes them for beginning this 'all-abhorred war' (16). Comparing the kingdom to the orderly heavens, he begs Worcester to take his place once more as a planet in its sphere, giving light, instead of behaving rebelliously, like a meteor, flashing across the sky and foretelling disasters (see page 34). At the very beginning of the play Worcester is described with the same metaphor as being 'malevolent to you [the King] in all aspects' (I.i.96) – that is, a planet shedding evil influence.

Worcester protests that he has not sought this battle, and Falstaff chips in with the excuse of a thief caught with stolen goods: 'Rebellion lay in his way, and he found it' (28), only to be silenced by the Prince. But Falstaff's presence makes us aware that the worlds of court and tavern, so far apart when the play began, have met.

Worcester tries to justify their rebellion by repeating again the account of Bolingbroke's return, which Hotspur had recounted to Blunt. Worcester points out that it was the Percys who welcomed back the exiled Bolingbroke, when he swore that he came only for his own rightful inheritance, his father's land, which the King had seized. But 'such a flood of greatness' (48) fell on Bolingbroke, circumstances pushed him on to become King; then he forgot his debt to the Percys and oppressed them. Bitterness pervades Worcester's speech, and the King replies in a similar tone, that these accusations can only lead to a continuing time of 'pell-mell havoc and confusion' (82).

The deadlock is broken by Hal, who offers to save much bloodshed by fighting Hotspur in single combat. (In 1591, at the siege of Rouen, the Earl of Essex offered to fight Villars, governor of Rouen, in single combat, and as late as the 1640s the Duke of Newcastle wanted to settle the Civil War by fighting a duel with Sir Thomas Fairfax.) Hal courteously says that he joins 'with all the world In praise of Harry Percy' (86) and his 'noble deeds' (92), and modestly confesses that in contrast 'I have a truant been to chivalry' (94). The King forbids this trial of strength, but offers Worcester peace, with a complete amnesty to all the rebels, 'yea, every man Shall be my friend again, and I'll be his.. . . We offer fair; take it advisedly' (107, 114).

The envoys leave. The situation is both absurd and tragic; both sides really want peace. The King wishes to rule over a peaceful, united society; the rebels know they are likely to be defeated if they fight, but dare not trust the King.

The Prince thinks that the offer of peace will be rejected, because

> The Douglas and the Hotspur both together
> Are confident against the world in arms. (116)

Alone with the Prince, Falstaff tries to return to the old joking relationship: 'Hal, if thou see me down in the battle and bestride me, so! 'Tis a point of friendship' (121). But the Prince cannot idle now: 'Nothing but a colossus can do thee that friendship. Say thy prayers, and farewell' (123). Falstaff is almost pathetic: 'I would 'twere bedtime, Hal, and all well.' But the Prince has duties to perform, brushes him off, and flings, 'Why, thou owest God a death' over his shoulder, as he hurries out.

Even when alone, Falstaff has to pun, taking 'death' for 'debt' (pronounced the same way in Elizabethan times), he says, "'Tis not due yet: I would be loathe to pay him before his day' (127). He meditates on this curious thing 'honour', so prized by Hal and Hotspur, who are hastening to the battle field to gain it. But what is it worth to the ordinary man? Falstaff concludes that it is worth nothing (see page 37).

Act V, Scene ii

Immediately we hear Worcester trying to persuade Vernon not to pass on to Hotspur the King's 'liberal and kind offer' (2). Politician Worcester cannot believe that the King will keep his word; Worcester thinks that young, impetuous, 'hare-brained Hotspur' may be forgiven, but never his father and uncle.

Vernon agrees to this thoroughly dishonourable scheme, and Worcester simply declares to Hotspur that the battle will begin immediately, and that 'there is no seeming mercy in the King' (34). Hotspur typically responds, 'Did you beg any? God forbid!' (35).

When the challenge of the Prince of Wales is reported Hotspur is eager to know if it was made in contempt; far from it, Vernon assures him, and goes on with lavish praises of Hal, 'so much misconstrued in his wantonness' (68). Hotspur is amazed; he brushes aside the idea of the reformed Prince; whatever Hal may be, Hotspur is determined to overcome him. All the while claiming that he has not 'the gift of tongue' (77) and that 'I profess not talking' (91), Hotspur makes eloquent speeches to his fellow-rebels; it is ironic that the King's prayer: 'And God befriend us as our cause is just' (V.i.120) is echoed by Hotspur:

> Now, for our consciences, the arms are fair
> When the intent of bearing them is just. (87)

And though he shouts the Percy motto, 'Esperance!' [Hope!] yet Hotspur's farewell is sombre:

> Sound all the lofty instruments of war,
> And by that music let us all embrace;
> For, heaven to earth, some of us never shall
> A second time do such a courtesy. (97)

This is not the speech of a man confident of victory; much more like the words of a brave leader of a forlorn hope.

Act V, Scene iii

Shakespeare had no crowds of 'extras'; he never attempts to show the main encounter of two armies on the stage, but exhibits the skirmishes which happen on the outskirts of the action. To confuse the enemy, King Henry has several of his nobles wearing surcoats (sleeveless tunics) decorated with the royal coat-of-arms (faces were hidden by helmets). We first see

Douglas, boasting that he has already killed one 'likeness' (8) of the King, the Earl of Stafford. Now he challenges another, Sir Walter Blunt, and believing him to be the real King, kills him. Douglas hails Hotspur triumphantly: 'All's done, all's won; here breathless lies the King' (16), only to be told that this is merely the faithful Sir Walter Blunt.

Hotspur and Douglas hasten back to the fighting, and Falstaff enters, as usual talking wittily to himself. 'Though I could escape shot-free [without paying my bill, and unwounded] at London, I fear the shot here' (30). He recognises the dead Sir Walter and cries contemptuously 'There's honour for you!' Falstaff has directed his ragged soldiers to the hottest part of the fight, and they are virtually wiped out – so he can keep their pay.

Hal enters and recalls their early encounters in idleness: 'What, stands thou idle here? Lend me thy sword' (40). The Prince is not concerned about the fate of the common soldiers, but must revenge the dead nobles lying on the field. Falstaff offers him what is apparently a pistol in a case, but when the Prince pulls it out, it is a bottle of sack, which angers him; Falstaff's jokes are no longer funny. The Prince cries, 'What, is it a time to jest and dally now?' (56). Holiday is over.

Falstaff is left gazing at Sir Walter's body, with its grinning skull: 'I like not such grinning honour as Sir Walter hath. Give me life, which, if I can save, so; if not, honour comes unlooked for, and there's an end.' (59) 'Give me life'; is this ignoble, or is it simply the rational and sensible view of every ordinary man?

Act V, Scene iv

The original stage directions here say 'Alarms, excursions', that is, trumpet calls and skirmishes, soldiers chasing each other in and out and exchanging blows. The Prince is wounded, but refuses to leave the field, and goes off to fight once more. Douglas finds the King alone, attacks him fiercely, and is overcoming him, when the Prince of Wales runs in and beats off Douglas, who flees.

The King declares that this rescue shows that Hal actually wants to keep him alive, and Hal then realises just how much he has made his father mistrust him, and indignantly protests. The Prince's high valour is Shakespeare's addition; the *Chronicles* report only that 'he helped his father like a lusty young gentleman'.

Now comes the first and last meeting of the two Harrys (also invented by Shakespeare). They have been compared continually throughout the play; at last they are face to face. Both realise that this is a crucial encounter:

> Two stars keep not their motion in one sphere,
> Nor can one England brook a double reign
> Of Harry Percy and the Prince of Wales. (64)

Hotspur still thinks the Prince a wastrel and an unworthy opponent, and regrets that Hal is so much less famous as a warrior – hardly worth fighting. The Prince repeats what he vowed to his father:

> . . .all the budding honours on thy crest
> I'll crop to make a garland for my head. (71)

While they fight, Falstaff comes in and watches, until Douglas enters and attacks him, when Falstaff falls down as if dead, and Douglas goes off after other conquests.

Prince Hal defeats Hotspur, who laments the loss of his 'proud titles' even more than his life. There is an intense sense of waste, and great pathos in Hotspur's exclamation: 'O Harry, thou hast robbed me of my youth!' (76). The Prince does not exult over his fallen rival, but clearly feels the tragedy of the extinction of so much promise and vitality:

> When that this body did contain a spirit,
> A kingdom for it was too small a bound;
> But now two paces of the vilest earth
> Is room enough. (88)

He solemnly covers the dead face with his 'favours' – possibly a scarf from his helmet – and speaks a last, generous farewell:

> Adieu, and take thy praise with thee to heaven.
> Thy ignominy sleep with thee in the grave,
> But not remembered in thy epitaph. (98)

Spying Falstaff's body, the Prince speaks an epitaph for him also, with mixed emotions, addressing him as 'acquaintance', not as 'friend' (101). There is pity for 'Poor Jack', but clear-eyed acknowledgement that only if the Prince was 'much in love with vanity' would he feel a 'heavy loss' in losing Falstaff. Hotspur received the tribute due to an equal; for Falstaff the responsible Prince will see that the body of his dependant, his court jester, is suitably embalmed.

The mood changes; to the astonishment and laughter of the audience Falstaff comes to life and heaves himself to his feet, most unwilling to be disembowelled and embalmed. He argues that to save one's life by counterfeiting is to be 'the true and perfect image of life indeed' (118).

But what if Percy, too, is not dead but counterfeiting? Falstaff immediately decides to try to get credit for killing Hotspur, and with superb insolence looks at the audience, saying, 'Nothing confutes me but eyes, and nobody sees me' (126). A good joke. But he then loses all our sympathy; he stabs the dead Hotspur. He is trying to lift up the dead body when disturbed by the Prince of Wales and Prince John.

Hal is congratulating his brother Prince John on the way he has 'fleshed' his 'maiden sword' (129) – a strong contrast to Sir John's ignoble stabbing of the dead – and then the Princes are astounded to see Falstaff, alive. Calmly Falstaff claims to have slain Percy, and for this, he declares, he should be ennobled.

Falstaff begins to weave a tale about his conquest of Hotspur, a blatant lie, just like the abundant inventions he poured out about the fight at Gadshill: 'we...fought a long hour by Shrewsbury clock' (147). But he is no longer in the tavern. The Prince has neither time nor inclination to listen; casually he assents to the ridiculous claim, and hastens off towards the sound of victorious trumpets. We note that, having killed Hotspur, he resigns the 'honour' to Falstaff, not requiring applause for himself.

Falstaff follows, dragging Hotspur's body, and promising amendment of life, as so often, and so vainly, before: 'If I do grow great, I'll grow less; for I'll purge, and leave sack, and live cleanly, as a nobleman should do' (163).

Act V, Scene v

The last scene shows the King rebuking Worcester. Rebellion has been put down, but at what cost. The lies told by 'ill-spirited Worcester' when he refused to tell Hotspur of the 'grace, pardon and terms of love' (2) offered by the King, have caused untold suffering. Worcester and Vernon are, inevitably, executed: 'Thus ever did rebellion find rebuke' (1). This is exactly the sentiment which Elizabeth's government sought to impress on her people, and repeated in the *Homilies* circulated to be read in churches.

Douglas has been captured, in slightly comical circumstances, and the Prince of Wales, now a model of chivalry, sends Prince John to release him without ransom, because of his valour and 'high deeds' (30).

But there is no comfortable 'happy ending' to the play. Prince John and Westmoreland must go to put down Northumberland and the Archbishop of York; the King and the Prince of Wales, reconciled, must fight with Glendower and the Earl of March. 'Rebellion in this land shall lose his sway' (41), says the King, the most orthodox of Elizabethan wishes, and Shakespeare will show this happening in his next play, *Henry IV Part II*, which will also complete the education of the Prince of Wales.

4 THEMES AND ISSUES

4.1 ORDER AND DISORDER

To enjoy Shakespeare's history plays it is necessary to have some idea of the Elizabethan 'world-picture', which was very different from our own. We regard the chaotic state of the political world as 'natural', whereas to an Elizabethan a dis-ordered war-torn state was definitely 'everything that seems un-natural' (*Henry V*, V.ii.62).

They believed that God had created, and desired, an orderly universe. The 'huge firm earth' (*King John*, III.i.72) was in the centre, and round it the sun and the planets circled, each in its crystal sphere, each sounding its own note of music, combining in heavenly harmony. And this concord, they thought, should be reflected on earth. Government could be compared to music:

> For government, though high and low and lower,
> Put into parts, doth keep in one consent,
> Congreeing in a full and natural close,
> Like music.   (*Henry V*, I.ii.189)

The universe was one and indivisible:

> The Heavens themselves, the planets and this centre [the earth]
> Observe degree, priority and place, (*Troilus and Cressida*, I.iii.85)

and so should men likewise.

Rebellion, with civil war, was, of course, the worst form of dis-order. Henry IV begs Worcester to leave rebellion and return to his proper place, as a planet moving in its correct orbit, rather than be a random meteor, a portent of evil (V.i.15–20). Unfavourable stars brought dis-asters. And however different their aims, Falstaff and Hotspur are each trying to demolish established authority.

4.2 REBELLION

The official Tudor view of the events of the fifteenth century was that because of the sacrilegious murder of Richard II there had been almost continuous strife, culminating in the defeat of the wicked King Richard III by the first Tudor King, Henry VII, and that he had brought peace and prosperity to England. In fact, the Tudors had to deal with many rebellions and risings, the latest the Northern Rising of 1569, led by the Percys – the family who rebel in *Henry IV Part I*. When the Earl of Essex rebelled in 1601, there were two members of the Percy family among his followers. Elizabethans had only to look across the Channel to see in France the horrors of civil war.

Tudor monarchs had very little physical power, and no standing army or police force, so to keep order they emphasised the wickedness of rebellion and the religious duty of obedience. St Paul had said, 'The powers that be are ordained of God. . .they that resist shall receive to themselves damnation' (*Romans*, xiii.1). In Shakespeare's plays rebellion is 'gross' and 'foul' (*Richard II*, II.ii.109): III.ii.26), 'damn'd commotion' (*Henry IV Part II*, IV.i.32); the 'due meet for rebellion' is instant death (*Henry IV Part II*, IV.ii.17), and 'rebellious hinds' are 'filth and scum' (*Henry VI Part II*, IV.ii.130). Worcester complains that the King 'calls us rebels. . .this hateful name' (*Henry IV Part I*, V.ii.39).

Weekly church-going was compulsory in Elizabeth's reign, and the government circulated sermons known as *Homilies*, which were read in every church. Echoes of these *Homilies* occur frequently in Shakespeare's histories. The *Homily against Disobedience* stated, 'We must not in any wise withstand violently, or rebel. . .against the anointed of the Lord' – exactly what John of Gaunt and the Bishop of Carlisle say in *Richard II*: the King was God's 'deputy anointed in his sight' (I.ii.37-41; IV.i.121-31). *A Mirror for Magistrates* agrees: 'Whosoever rebelleth against any ruler either good or bad rebelleth against God and shall be sure of a wretched end, for God cannot but sustain his deputy.'

4.3 KINGSHIP

Monarchy was considered the best form of government, because ordained by God in the Scriptures. The king must control his subjects; better one tyrant than a weak king who allows many nobles to become petty tyrants. The relation of king and people was organic: 'never alone / Did the king sigh, but with a general groan' (*Hamlet*, III.iii.23).

The magic of kingship is hinted at when Falstaff declares that a lion (traditionally the king of beasts) will not attack a true prince, and that the same instinct prevented him from striking Prince Hal at Gadshill.

The king was divinely appointed to rule, but had to rule well and obey the laws, to do his best in the place which God had allotted to him. Men owed obedience to the king, as the king owed obedience to God. However bad a king might be, God was the only being who could displace him. In the early political play *Gorboduc* we read:

> Though kings forget to govern as they ought,
> Yet subjects must obey as they are bound - (V.i.42)

a very orthodox sentiment. Camillo in *The Winter's Tale* will not obey Leontes' order to kill King Polixenes, for of all those who have killed anointed kings, none 'flourish'd after' (I.ii.359).

Elizabethan religious and political thought are inseparable. The deposing of King Richard II, followed by his murder, is not only a crime, but a deadly sin, and therefore the reign of the new King, Henry IV, is bound to be disturbed. The play of *Richard II* ends with the new King vowing:

> I'll make a voyage to the Holy Land
> To wash this blood off from my guilty hand. (V.vi.49)

but even a year later, when *Henry IV Part I* begins, continual unrest in the kingdom has prevented any crusade. And we are three times reminded, in *Henry IV Part I*, at length, by Hotspur and Worcester, how Henry got the crown (I.iii.158-84; IV.iii.52-105; V.i.32-71); we also hear Henry's own confession (III.ii.39-84).

Shakespeare does not deal with these political ideas in the abstract, but illustrates them through individual men. Richard II had divine sanction as a king, but his frivolous, wasteful character made him a bad ruler. Henry IV had the necessary political qualities, and truly desired to be a good king and unite his country, but his flawed claim to the throne led to constant uprisings against him. The regicide was afraid of being slain, the usurper of having his crown usurped by his son. He also regarded his son's wanton behaviour as a punishment from God for Richard's deposition (III.ii.4-11).

Hal is coolly looking forward to becoming king; educating himself by getting to know all kinds of people, quite well aware that this temporary way of life must come to an abrupt stop, but enjoying it while it lasts.

4.4 HONOUR

During the 1590s many tracts were published in praise of Elizabethan generals and admirals who were harassing the Spaniards by land and sea, and these tracts placed great emphasis on the 'honour' to be gained in such enterprises. Courtiers were exhorted to leave 'soft unprofitable pleasures' and earn 'true honour' in the field; 'scorning the idle life' and holding 'honour in greater regard than ease at home'.

George Peele, the playwright, wrote typical verses on this theme. In honour of Sir Francis Drake in 1589:

> All honours do this cause accompany;
> All glory on these endless honours waits;

and to welcome home the Earl of Essex from Portugal in the same year:

> O honour's fire, that not the brackish sea
> Might quench, nor foemen's fearful 'larums lay!

The word 'honour' echoes through *Henry IV Part I*. Hotspur is called 'the theme of honour's tongue' (I.i.80), the 'child of honour and renown' (III.ii.139), and the 'king of honour' (IV.i.10). His Scots prisoners are 'an honourable spoil' (I.i.74) and his fight against Douglas gains him 'never-dying honour' (III.ii.106). He cannot understand the lord who withdraws from 'so honourable an action' as their conspiracy (II.iii.33) and tells his father and uncle that they can 'redeem [their] banished honours' by standing up to the King (I.iii.178). No danger is too great if only he can gather 'honour' from it (I.iii.194, 200, 203).

While Hotspur fights, the Prince sports with drawers in the cellar, and mockingly tells Poins that he has 'lost much honour, that thou wast not with me in this action' (II.iv.21). But in the next scene the King taunts the Prince with Hotspur's 'never-dying honour' (acquired, oddly enough, by leading 'ancient lords and reverent bishops on to bloody battles' [III.ii.104]), and Hal retorts seriously that he will meet and vanquish Hotspur, 'child of honour and renown' though he is (III.ii.139), and take over 'every honour sitting on his helm' (III.ii.142).

Even sober Vernon, challenged by Douglas, says he knows no fear 'if well-respected honour bid me on' (IV.iii.10). All these well-born characters are willing to shed blood, their own and that of others, for 'honour'.

Falstaff's point of view is completely different (V.i.129). In a famous speech (which Samuel Pepys, the diarist, thought the best thing in the play) he meditates on this curious thing 'honour'. In war 'honour pricks [spurs] me *on*'. But then what if his name is pricked *off* (as dead) on the muster list? He proceeds with a 'catechism' like the series of questions and answers through which children were taught religious beliefs. What can honour do? It cannot set a broken leg, nor an arm, nor relieve the pain of a wound. It is a word, made of nothing but air. The dead cannot take it with them; malicious tongues take it from the living. It is worth nothing, a 'mere scutcheon', which was a coat-of-arms painted on paper, buckram or thin wood, carried in a funeral procession, which looked like a shield, but was in fact too fragile to protect anyone.

'Honour' to Falstaff is totally worthless. On the battlefield he finds the body of Sir Walter Blunt, who has given his life for the King: 'There's honour for you!' is Falstaff's comment. 'I like not such grinning honour as Sir Walter hath. Give me life' (V.iii.32, 59).

Shakespeare leaves it to the audience to decide which valuation to accept.

4.5 'REDEEMING TIME'

In *Henry IV Part I* the word 'honour' is used twenty-nine times, but the word 'time' not only appears forty-one times, it is also constantly referred to in other words. Shakespeare makes their use of time a measure of his kings; Richard II, the failure, realises that 'I wasted time, and now doth time waste me' (*Richard II*, V.v.49); but the model king, Henry V, 'weighs time, even to the upmost grain' (*Henry V*, II.iv.137).

The good and prudent use of time was the subject of many Elizabethan religious works, which emphasised the impossibility of making up for lost time. St Paul's message to the Ephesians, that they should 'walk circumspectly. . .redeeming the time', that is, using it as well as possible, was widely quoted, and echoed when Prince Hal tells the audience that this is what he plans to do 'when men think least I will' (I.ii.222).

Falstaff is introduced to us asking the time of day, only to be told that he has no need to know it, because he steals or revels all night, and sleeps all day. He embodies Idleness – which in the *Homily* against it was called 'a grievous sin' – and the lazy tempo of life in the tavern is contrasted with the bustle of the court scenes, where the harassed king is beseiged with business: 'Come yourself with speed to us again' he cries to Westmoreland, 'For more is to be said and to be done' (I.i.104).

In the tavern there is time to joke, to drink with the drawers, to tell tall tales, to act plays extempore (making fun of these busy men, Hotspur and the King), time for Falstaff to snore behind the arras. But when the king sends for the Prince, and he, asking the time, is told 'two o'clock', he bids Peto, 'Be with me betimes in the morning' (II.iv.536, 560). Then in the morning, reconciled to the king, he is hurried off:

> Our hands are full of business. Let's away.
> Advantage feeds him fat while men delay. (III.ii.179)

The Prince's last visit to the tavern is only to give marching orders to Falstaff, and he leaves in haste crying 'to horse, to horse' (III.iii.203).

Time presses on all politicians, including the rebels. It is sheer love of battle that makes Hotspur cry, 'O let the hours be short till fields and blows and groans applaud our sport' (I.iii.196). But when one of the conspirators drops out, this compels them to push on quickly, lest he tell the King their plans. The 'hot Lord Percy is on fire to go' (III.i.264) and cannot understand how his father has 'the leisure to be sick in such a justling time' (IV.i.17). Northumberland says that he cannot send his forces 'so soon' (IV.i.33), but they hear that the King is coming 'speedily' and that Glendower cannot join them for 'fourteen days' (IV.i.33, 92, 126). Hotspur can only 'take a muster speedily', though he knows that they are rushing on to destruction: 'Doomsday is near!' (IV.i.133)

We see the rebel leaders once more at odds with each other: Hotspur insisting that they fight immediately, despite their doubtful strength, while the King comes on with 'mighty and quick-raisèd power' (IV.iv.12).

No one in politics can escape the pressure of time. The rebel Archbishop of York bids Sir Michael distribute his messages to the other set of conspirators 'with winged haste', 'make haste. . .to prevent the worst, Sir Michael, speed. . .make haste' (IV.iv.2, 5, 35, 40).

Falstaff, on the other hand, proceeds to battle in a typically leisurely way, and is rebuked by Westmoreland, ''Tis more than time that I were [at Shrewsbury] and you too. . .we must away all night'. But neither this, nor the Prince's 'Sirrah, make haste' move Falstaff; to arrive at the *latter* end of a fray will suit him admirably (IV.ii.55, 75, 80). When he does appear on the battlefield Falstaff is completely out of place. He offers the Prince a pistol case, which in fact contains a bottle of sack [sweet wine] and is scornfully dismissed: 'What, is it a time to jest and dally now?' (V.iii.56) Not for the Prince; holiday-time is over and there is deadly work to be done; but for Falstaff it is still a 'time to counterfeit', this time to counterfeit death to escape the Douglas.

For Hal and Hotspur it is the moment of truth, the climax of their rivalry. They fight in single combat. For Hal, 'the time [has] come that I shall make this northern youth exchange his glorious deeds for my indignities'; true to his boast to his father he does make Percy 'render every glory up' (III.ii.144, 150). Hotspur has only seconds left to address time:

> But thoughts, the slaves of life, and life, time's fool,
> And time, that takes survey of all the world,
> Must have a stop.   (V.iv.80)

In the end, it is not the King, but Hotspur's father, Northumberland, who will have to say of his son, 'The hope and expectation of thy time is ruined' (III.ii.36).

Any history play inevitably belongs to a sequence of events; Shakespeare reminds us of the happenings which preceded, and shaped, the events of

Henry IV Part I.

Worcester reminds the King that he owes his throne to the Percys' support (I.iii.12; V.i.33), and that as Henry Bolingbroke, returning from exile, he had sworn that he came for nothing more than his father's dukedom. Hotspur, blazing with rage, recalls how this 'vile politician, Bolingbroke' (I.iii.238) had fawned on him when returning from exile, but now as King orders him to surrender his prisoners, and refuses to ransom Mortimer. The King remembers how he managed to ingratiate himself with the people, and to 'pluck allegiance from men's hearts. . .even in the presence of the crowned king [Richard]' (III.ii.52).

The humbler comrades have been together for a long time; Falstaff has paid for Bardolph's drinks for thirty-two years (III.iii.49). And long, long before, Falstaff was thin, and 'could have crept into any alderman's thumb-ring' (II.iv.337) – perhaps a recollection of Shakespeare's father, alderman of Stratford-upon-Avon.

A sense of time relentlessly advancing pervades the play: Falstaff dreams of Hal's accession, and five times in one scene repeats, 'when thou art king' (I.ii.16, 23, 63, 65, 151). The Prince himself bides his time, but knows that one day he will appear 'redeeming time when men think least I will' (I.ii.222), when at last he and Hotspur meet face to face in battle.

5 TECHNICAL FEATURES

5.1 CHARACTERISATION

Falstaff

The combination of historical events with scenes from everyday life, plus a great comic figure, made *Henry IV Part I* a new kind of play. Falstaff was at once a tremendous success. It is said that Queen Elizabeth I was so delighted with him that she asked for another play showing the fat knight in love, so Shakespeare wrote *The Merry Wives of Windsor.* In the first printed version of *Henry IV Part I* in 1598, the title page promised readers 'the humorous conceits of Sir John Falstaff' as an inducement to buy.

Of all Shakespeare's characters he is the one most frequently mentioned in seventeenth-century writings; between 1599 and 1700 there are nearly a hundred allusions to Falstaff (five times as many as to Hamlet), occurring, for instance, in letters from the Countess of Southampton in 1559 and the Duchess of Newcastle in 1644, in a play by Ben Jonson in 1599 and in a play by William Wycherley in 1675. There are references to thin theatre audiences in the seventeenth-century playhouses, except when Falstaff appeared and drew the crowds, and the throng stopped cracking nuts to listen to him. In the eighteenth century Dr Samuel Johnson described him as 'unimitated, unimitable', and the essayist William Hazlitt in the nine-teenth century declared that Falstaff was 'perhaps the most substantial comic character that ever was invented'.

There is no doubt that Falstaff spends his time in thieving, cheating, lying, bragging, lechery, cowardice and taking bribes; but at the same time he is vital, quick-thinking, witty, eloquent and (in this play) altogether life-enhancing.

Falstaff is not merely a buffoon. He is intelligent and has had some classical education: he calls the sun 'Phoebus' (I.ii.16) and himself 'valiant as Hercules' (II.iv.276). The hostess is hailed as 'Dame Partlet the hen' (III.iii.55) from Chaucer, and Bardolph's red nose makes him 'the Knight of the Burning Lamp' (III.iii.28), parodying '*Amadis, Knight of the Burning Sword*.

Falstaff was originally called Sir John Oldcastle, after a real friend of King Henry V. An Elizabethan descendant of the real Sir John's wife objected strongly, and the name was changed. A rival dramatic company put on a play about the real Oldcastle, stating, 'It is no pampered glutton we present. . .'.

The real Oldcastle was a Protestant martyr, which may have suggested to Shakespeare a man with much biblical knowledge. Falstaff is forever making biblical references, to Lazarus and Dives (IV.ii.25; III.iii.29; *Luke*, xvi.19), for instance, to Pharoah's lean kine (II.iv.256; *Genesis*, xii.19), to the Prodigal Son (IV.ii.34; *Luke*, xv.15). Falstaff misquotes the Scriptures for his own purposes, as 'Watch tonight, pray tomorrow' (II.iv.283) for 'Watch and pray, that you enter not into temptation' (*Matthew*, xxvi.41), and facetiously wishes himself a Puritan weaver, singing psalms (II.iv.34).

Falstaff makes frequent empty declarations of repentance ('Monsieur Remorse', Poins calls him [I.ii.118]); 'I prithee trouble me no more with vanity' (I.ii.86); 'I must give over this life and I will give it over' (I.ii.101); 'Well, I'll repent' (III.iii.5); 'I'll purge, and leave sack and live cleanly' (V.iv.164).

His assumption of repentance and piety is as unreal as his boasts of prowess in battle. But can his outrageously false remarks be called lies? While still wiping his lips from his last drink, he calls for more: 'Give me a cup of sack. *I am a rogue* if I drunk today' (II.iv.154). Obviously he does not expect to be believed then, nor when he describes the fight with the men in buckram: '*I am a rogue* if I were not at halfsword with them two hours together' (II.iv.167). And equally absurd is his claim to perpetual youth: 'They hate us youth', 'Young men must live' (II.ii.86, 92).

Falstaff's wits are sharp, his creative imagination for ever flowing, pouring out endearments, abuse, tall tales, in an unending stream. The Prince agrees to take part in the robbery so that he and Poins can laugh at the 'incomprehensible lies' which Falstaff will tell afterwards (I.ii.191).

Poins rightly surmises that Falstaff will fight no 'longer than he sees reason' (I.ii.189), and this describes admirably Falstaff's behaviour at Shrewsbury as well as at Gadshill. It was, to Falstaff, extremely reasonable merely to exchange a blow or two, and then to sham dead to avoid the Douglas' sword: 'Give me life' (V.iii.60).

Falstaff is irrepressible. Even while the battle is raging he has to claim ludicrously that he is as brave as 'Turk Gregory' (the Grand Turk and Pope Gregory XIII appeared in a colour print in 1579 as two of 'The Three Tyrants of the World'). Falstaff offers the Prince a bottle of sack instead of a weapon, and puns absurdly that he will 'pierce' Percy (V.iii.57).

So far, so good. But when, in a parody of military valour, Falstaff stabs the dead Hotspur, he alienates us. This is no joking matter. He has gone too far and seems, for the moment at least, totally ignoble.

Tastes change. At a performance in the 1760s 'no joke ever raised such loud repeated mirth in the galleries as Sir John's labour in getting the body of Percy on his back'.

As well as reminding us of the Vice (see page 71), Falstaff resembles another traditional figure, the Lord of Misrule. During the twelve days of Christmas, as during the Roman Saturnalia, the Lord of Misrule held sway and everything was topsy-turvy, chaotic and disordered. The clergy disapproved of such goings-on, but the custom was clearly widespread, since 'visitations' were sent to Norwich, York, Lichfield and Oxford, and to London in 1601, to ensure that 'any lords of misrule' did not 'come irreverently into the church or churchyard'. Falstaff does indeed live in perpetual disorder, 'out of all order, out of all compass' (III.iii.21) and his immense bulk is symbolic. The ideas of waste, extravagance and excess are literally embodied in him. He answers the Prince's teasing 'Sir John Paunch' (II.ii.66) with 'I am not John of Gaunt your grandfather' – reminding us of John of Gaunt's dying words,

> For sleeping England long time have I watched,
> Watching breeds leanness, leanness is all gaunt.
> (*Richard II*, II.i.77)

Falstaff uses his bulk as an ever-present source of jokes and ingenious excuses: 'I have more flesh than another man, and therefore more frailty' (III.iii.173).

The Prince is both fascinated and disgusted by Falstaff's size. When acting the part of King Henry, Hal hurls abuse, frightening in its intensity, at Falstaff (II.iv.456–73), and throughout he calls him by such names as tallow, butter, fat-guts, fat-kidneyed rascal, brawn [a fat pig ready for slaughter], 'this horse-back breaker', 'this huge hill of flesh', 'gross as a mountain'. This hurling of abuse at each other without subsequent ill-feeling is a predominantly masculine custom – illustrated also by Falstaff's abuse of Bardolph, which in no way prevented Bardolph's deep grief at Falstaff's death (*Henry V*, II.iii.7).

The most important thing in Falstaff's life is his relationship with the Prince – they appear together in eight scenes and for over nine hundred lines. Falstaff longs to take the place of Hal's estranged father, the King, and his devotion is obvious from their first appearance, with his repeated endearments: 'lad', 'sweet wag', 'mad wag', 'sweet young prince'. Falstaff wishes not only for material benefits 'when thou art king', but longs for some return of affection: 'thy love is worth a million, thou owest me thy love' (III.iii.141). But he pleads in vain.

In the play-acting scene Falstaff tries to present himself as a suitable father-figure for the Prince: 'A goodly portly man...a most noble carriage...there is virtue in that Falstaff' (II.iv.431), and begs not to be banished, only to be slapped down with the cold 'I do. I will' (II.iv.291). Falstaff pleads 'an [if] thou lovest me' (II.iv.289), but to everyone except Falstaff himself it is obvious that the Prince has no warmer feeling for him than could be felt for an amusing acquaintance, and that Falstaff will be discarded with the others when the right moment comes. Falstaff, so quick-witted in all other situations, is 'fat-witted' in this most vital one. He cannot believe that moment will come (as described by Shakespeare in his Sonnet 49):

> ...that time when thou shalt strangely pass
> And scarcely greet me with that sun, thine eye.

At one level Falstaff may be Hal's tempter or evil angel, but Shakespeare uses him also as a commentator, giving the view of the man in the street. Falstaff collects an army of down-and-outs by allowing better men to bribe him to let them stay at home; the miserable rabble are 'food for powder' to 'fill a pit'; why risk 'good householders, yeomen's sons' (IV.ii.76, 15) in so foolish an enterprise as civil war? 'I like not such grinning honour as Sir Walter hath. Give me life' (V.iii.59).

'This is the strangest fellow', says the Prince (V.iv.158). Falstaff obeys no conventions. He simply ignores everything inconvenient: debts, duty, conscience, morality, law and order. Always he puts himself first. He cheats the King when recruiting, and the Hostess in Eastcheap. He eats and drinks with gusto – but we never see him incapably drunk, or sick, or slow-witted. We do see him getting into difficulties – for instance we know that the Prince is fully aware of the true story of Gadshill, and Falstaff, we think, telling such outrageous lies, must be cornered. But behold, he triumphantly explains that he was 'a coward on instinct', complimenting Hal on being a 'true prince', and all ends in laughter.

Editing Shakespeare in the eighteenth century, Dr Samuel Johnson said that Falstaff has 'perpetual gaiety...an unfailing power of exciting laughter'. We laugh both with and at Falstaff; he enjoys everything; he jests to himself when there is no one else about, enjoying his own company. We are carried away by his exuberance, and in the theatre we are not given time to dwell on his less attractive characteristics, which will be much more memorably exhibited in *Henry IV Part II*.

Prince Hal

The stability, health and wealth of a kingdom was thought to depend largely on the wisdom and strength of the king. Therefore it was import-ant that he should be well-brought-up in the broadest sense; and the right education of a prince was a subject of considerable importance to the Elizabethans. One of the themes of *Henry IV Part I* is the education of Prince Hal. But Prince Hal is unlike the 'Youth' of the interludes, misled by Riot and Luxury, who has to be reformed and undergoes a spiritual change, because he is never shown as debauched.

In an early *Chronicle* Prince Hal was given 'greatly to riot' and 'applied him unto all vice and insolency' with 'rioters and wild disposed persons'. Shakespeare's Hal, however, is never shown as gluttonous, drunk, lecherous or murderous, and the one time he indulges in highway robbery (*once* in my days I'll be a madcap' [I.ii.148]) he robs the robbers and returns the stolen money 'with advantage' (II.iv.540). The worst thing that can be imputed to him is 'vanity' - futile wasting of time, a serious fault in a prince - but this is not a deadly sin.

But the question does arise, whether Hal's playboy persona is as calculated and artificial as his father's 'courtesy' and 'humility' when Henry was planning to supplant King Richard (III.ii.50). Hal's planned reformation may be simply a political manoeuvre to 'show more goodly and attract more eyes', to impress the public (I.ii.219). And when he bitterly compares himself as 'your *un-thought-of* Harry' with 'this gallant Hotspur, this *all-praisèd* knight', again he refers to the public image of each (III.ii.140).

The change in Hal's behaviour is first promised in *Richard II* when the new King Henry IV sees 'some sparkles of a better hope' in his 'dissolute and desperate' son (V.iii.20). In Hal's first soliloquy, these 'sparkles' are a steady flame. The banishment of Falstaff is more than a joke when they act in the tavern (II.iv.291), and the Prince promises the King that he will mend his ways (III.ii). The transformed warrior Prince is described by Vernon (IV.i.97) and shown to us throughout the battle.

At the end of the first scene in which he appears, Hal makes it clear that his time in the tavern is a holiday, and holidays can last only a short time. His tavern days are numbered. But during them he has learnt how to get on with ordinary citizens, so that later as Henry V he can command 'all the good lads in Eastcheap' (II.iv.14) and, looking back on his 'wilder days' consider 'what use we made of them' (*Henry V*, I.ii.25). Hal is training for his inevitable destiny - to be a king. Falstaff has no future; he lives in the present moment, with the Prince paying his tavern bills in exchange for wit and laughter; he dreams hazily of a golden time 'when thou art king', when thieves will not be hanged, when both 'old father antic the law' and King Henry IV will be dead, and when he will indeed be the father-figure for his 'sweet young prince', at last on the throne. (I.ii.16, 23, 63, 65, 85).

Falstaff refuses to recognise the occasions when his warmth meets with a chill reception. After Falstaff's splendid tale of the Gadshill fight there comes, like a douche of cold water, the Prince's 'Hear me speak but this. . . a plain tale shall put you down ' (II.iv.256), followed by the bare facts.

Falstaff's imagination, when he prepares to act the part of the king, transforms his 'properties', but to the Prince, 'Thy state is taken for a joint stool, thy golden sceptre for a leaden dagger, and thy precious rich crown for a pitiful bald crown' (II.iv.387). Falstaff is 'put down' again when he begs never to be banished, and the Prince replies 'I do. I will' (II.iv.291).

Falstaff is genuinely curious when he asks the Prince, faced with Douglas, Percy and Glendower, 'Art thou not horrible afeard?' The Prince truly replies, 'Not a whit, i'faith. I lack some of thy instinct' (II.iv.373). He is needling Falstaff yet again about Gadshill, but also defining the difference between them; Falstaff lives by instinct, the Prince by reason.

Each is very conscious of the other's size. Falstaff's epithets are comic: 'you starveling, you eel-skin, you dried meat's tongue, you bull's pizzle. . . you tailor's yard, you sheath, you bow-case, you vile standing tuck [a long narrow rapier set up on end]' (II.iv.249). The Prince's descriptions are disgusting and cruel: 'clay-brained guts. . .whoreson obscene greasy tallow-catch. . .bolting-hutch of beastliness,. . .swollen parcel of dropsies,. . . stuffed cloak-bag of guts' (II.iv.231).

Hal is amused by Falstaff, and likes him well enough to support Falstaff's lie about killing Hotspur. But the Prince does not seem to have strong feelings for anyone but his father. He is really stung by his father's reproof and by the repeated insinuation that Hal might join the Percys to oust the king: 'Do not think so, you shall not find it so' and

> O God they did me too much injury
> That ever said I hearkened for your death,
>
> (III.ii.129; V.iv.50)

are heartfelt cries.

Hal and Hotspur are compared throughout (see page 72). Their temperaments are opposite. Hal is always a little detached, cool and calculating, able to wait till the moment for action arrives. Hotspur is foolhardy, hot-tempered, impulsive, outspoken, and must always be doing immediately whatever enters his head. Hal is politic; Hotspur thinks politicians 'vile' (I.iii.238).

Though to the modern reader Hal may seem a central figure in the play, he is not mentioned on the title-pages of the early editions of *Henry IV Part I*, which pick out the King, Hotspur and Falstaff. Hal is enigmatical, and the other principal characters do not understand him. His father mistrusts him and suffers great anxiety on his account; Falstaff mistakes the Prince's 'holiday' for his permanent way of life, and will suffer rejection; Hotspur thinks Hal a 'nimble-footed madcap', and is killed by him in single combat (IV.i.95). Hal passes triumphantly on to become King Henry V, 'the mirror of all Christian kings' (*Henry V*, II.Prol.6).

Harry Percy (Hotspur)

Hotspur is the son of the Earl of Northumberland and the nephew of the Earl of Worcester. Hal calls Hotspur 'this northern youth' (III.ii.145) and indeed the Percys virtually ruled the north of England, where there was a saying that the North knew no Prince but a Percy. Hotspur has the unself-conscious arrogance of the highly-born, physically strong, wealthy young man, who has always been the most important person among his peers.

At first sight Hotspur is attractive, frank, eloquent and apparently reasonable. When the King demands his prisoners, Hotspur describes what happened. We sympathise with his scorn of the 'popinjay', the soft, silly courtier trying to patronise and dictate to the man who had just fought and won a major battle. It appears that the King's estimate of Hotspur as 'the theme of honour's tongue' (I.i.80) may be justified. But Hotspur does not give any reasons for his disobedience, nor will he surrender the prisoners.

When the King is not moved by his defence of Mortimer, and Hotspur sees that he will not get his own way, he becomes (as his father says) 'drunk with choler [rage]' and rants and raves (I.iii.127). The King has forbidden him to mention his brother-in-law, Mortimer (a claimant to the throne), so Hotspur threatens:

> . . .But I will find him when he lies asleep,
> And in his ear I'll holla 'Mortimer!' (I.iii.219)

This is amusing, but childish. Because Hotspur loses control, his wily uncle Worcester can easily appeal to his 'imagination of some great exploit' (I.iii.197) and persuade him into rash rebellion. Hotspur cares only for military glory, and is so uninterested in the political results that, going to a meeting to plan the division of the kingdom, he forgets the essential map.

Hotspur is straightforward and honest. There is nothing in him of the 'vile politician'. He is as much amazed as angry when a lord who has joined them backs out, and is staggered when his father Northumberland is afraid to bring his forces to Shrewsbury.

Touchy and quick to anger himself, he is unwilling to consider the feelings of others, neither those of his wife nor of his Welsh host, Glendower. When he ignores his wife's anxious pleas to be told his plans, is Hotspur callous, or is it that he cannot trust any woman, or that he can only think of one thing at a time? He objects to his wife's lady-like oath, 'in sooth' (III.i.246) and to a courtier's 'holiday and lady terms' (I.iii.45), but is careless how his own speech offends; tactlessly he nags and insults Glendower, mocking his belief in astrology and expressing strong dislike of poetry, music and the Welsh language – all things dear to Glendower's heart. And he does this at a time when it is essential to have good relations between the rebel leaders.

There are only three characters in Shakespeare's plays who express disbelief in astrology (the others are Edmund in *King Lear* and Cassius in *Julius Caesar*) and it is notable that all three are rebels, bent on upsetting order and authority.

Some indication of the Elizabethan view of Hotspur is given in Beaumont and Fletcher's play, *The Knight of the Burning Pestle*. An apprentice, Ralph, is showing his prowess as an actor; he is told to 'speak a huffing part' - that is, a blustering, hectoring part - and obliges with a garbled version of Hotspur's

> By heavens, methinks it were an easy leap
> To pluck bright honour from the pale-faced moon. (I.iii.199)

Hotspur's 'huffing', his recklessness and lack of consideration, is seen when he picks a quarrel with his colleagues about his share of the kingdom, and when they accede to his wishes, declares 'I do not care. . .but in the way of bargain. . .I'll cavil on the ninth part of a hair' (III.i.145). At Shrewsbury Hotspur is so keen to fight at once that he ignores reports that his troops and horses are exhausted, and that certain reinforcements have not yet arrived.

When honest Sir Walter Blunt appears with offers of pardon from the King, Hotspur softens for a moment:

> BLUNT   I would you would accept of grace and love.
> HOTSPUR And may be so we shall. (IV.iii.112)

If next morning Worcester had truly reported 'the liberal and kind offer of the King' (V.ii.2) would Hotspur have made peace? But Worcester lies, and battle becomes inevitable.

Hotspur too truly says, 'The time of life is short' (V.ii.81), and so it proves for him. The inevitable clash of the two Harrys occurs, and the dying Hotspur's 'O Harry, thou hast robbed me of my youth!' brings home the horror of this senseless slaughter. For his epitaph we may quote an Elizabethan passage *On Honour*: 'The wisdom and discretion of a man is as great a virtue as his magnanimity and courage, which are so much the greater virtues, by how much they are accompanied with wisdom; for without them a man is not be be accounted valiant, but rather furious.'

In 1598 *Henry IV* was listed among Shakespeare's tragedies. If it is a tragedy, Hotspur is the tragic hero.

King Henry IV

In the play *Richard II*, Henry Bolingbroke appears as a strong, capable young nobleman, determined to regain the titles and lands of his father, John of Gaunt, Duke of Lancaster, which Richard has wrongfully seized. Other nobles, led by the Percys and afraid that the King might seize their property too, support Bolingbroke's claims, and apparently accept him as King Henry IV when Richard, unasked, abjectly surrenders the crown.

Only one year later, when *Henry IV Part I* begins, King Henry appears 'shaken. . .wan with care' (I.i.1) and apparently much older. Unlike the strong 'silent king' seen in *Richard II* dealing coolly with the emotional Richard and firmly with the quarrelling nobles, Henry now is clearly anxious, nervous, and angry because he hears that Hotspur will not surrender his prisoners. Later he peremptorily dismisses Worcester from the court and loses his temper with Northumberland and Hotspur.

King Henry longs to wipe out the past, to rule wisely and well, to lead a crusade to the Holy Land. But he is paying what was regarded as the inevitable price for dethroning an anointed king. He is tormented by guilt over Richard's death, by his own uncertain title to the crown, by rebellious nobles and by his own wild, unsatisfactory son. There seems to be a pattern: Henry the regicide tries to placate God, the king of kings, by going on a pilgrimage, but never manages to go because Henry the rebel is rebelled against; Henry the usurper is afraid that his son will usurp his throne. The King is dogged by his past; no one can forget how he got the crown, and that he himself was once a rebel.

The King's relations with the powerful Percy family are bad; Henry fears that having destroyed one king they may try to destroy another; they know this and fear that Henry will attempt to render them powerless. We are shown a disillusioned man; having got the throne he worked for so assiduously, he finds it has only brought him what the Chronicler Edward Hall describes as 'unquiet times'.

The Elizabethans thought that every king had 'two bodies'; one was of 'the king', the office-holder, whoever the man in that position might be, and it was undying; the other was that of the individual person who at a particular moment wore the crown. We are shown Henry in both capacities; as the ruler determined to keep order and rule well, and as the bitterly disappointed father comparing his idle boy to Henry Percy, Hotspur, 'sweet fortune's minion and her pride' (I.i.82).

In III, ii King and Prince come face to face, and Henry speaks both as King and as a father. He can only explain Hal's behaviour, he says, by thinking that it is God's punishment for his own 'mis-treadings'. He enlarges on the importance of one's public image, and we learn that King Richard's complaint of Bolingbroke's 'courtship to the common people' (*Richard II*, I.iv.24) was justified; Henry had worked hard to create the situation when

> '. . .Men would tell their children 'This is he!'
> Others would say 'Where? Which is Bolingbroke? (III.ii.48)

until Bolingbroke

> . . .did pluck allegiance from men's hearts
> Even in the presence of the crownèd king. (III.ii.52)

In contrast, Richard is pictured as 'the skipping king', lord of misrule, companioned by 'shallow jesters and rash bavin wits', who made himself so common that the people were 'with his presence glutted, gorged and full' - words showing King Henry's revulsion (III.ii.61, 84).

This is a king's lesson in political manoeuvering, but at the idea that his son is just like Richard the father's genuine feeling appears; he breaks down and weeps. Nevertheless he goes on with exaggerated praise of Hotspur, finally suggesting that his 'degenerate' son, his 'nearest and dearest enemy' will 'fight against me under Percy's pay' (III.ii.128, 123, 126).

The Prince's spirited, and indeed boastful, defence calms his father's fears for the moment, but the King cannot trust anyone, and he seems almost surprised when later, on the field of battle, Hal does not leave him to be killed, but saves his life.

Who rides a tiger cannot dismount; Henry seized the throne and from that time had little choice of action, but was governed, as he says in *Henry IV Part II*, as all politicians are, by 'necessity'.

Mortimer

Roger Mortimer, Earl of March, was named by Richard II as his heir, and when the Earl died his son, Edmund, became the claimant to the throne. His uncle, Sir Edmund Mortimer, whose sister Elizabeth (called 'Kate' by Shakespeare) married Hotspur, was captured by Glendower. King Henry refused to ransom him, so he changed sides and married Glendower's daughter. Shakespeare, like his sources, confuses the two Edmund Mortimers, making Lady Percy at one point call Mortimer 'my brother Mortimer' (II.iii.82), but making Mortimer call her 'my aunt Percy', as if he was the Earl of March (III.i.194). It is of no importance; Mortimer does little more than provide a motive for Hotspur's rage and the Percys' rebellion, when at the beginning of the play the King refuses to ransom him. Hotspur gives this to Sir Walter Blunt as a reason for rebellion (IV.iv.93). But he tells Sir Walter not to report it to the King; Worcester's long complaint the next morning does not even mention Mortimer.

Shakespeare uses the polite, thoughtful manner of Mortimer, during the conspirators' meeting, as a contrast to Hotspur's brash behaviour. Mortimer provides a scene both touching and slightly comic when his devoted lady can only express her love by embraces - 'My wife can speak no English, I no Welsh' (III.i.191). Again, their relationship is contrasted with the rough joking of Hotspur and his Kate.

Though Mortimer seems to set off for Shrewsbury, he does not appear at the battle (as the Archbishop of York notes [IV.iv.23]) and we only hear of him again at the very end of the play, when the King and the Prince of Wales plan further campaigns against Glendower. Mortimer's name is not mentioned in *Henry IV Part II* nor in *Henry V*; but as Mortimer dies in *Henry VI Part I*, a weak exhausted prisoner in the Tower of London, he recounts the whole story of Richard's deposition, and attributes the Percys' rebellion to their desire to see him on the throne (II.v.61-92).

Bardolph and the Hostess (Mistress Quickly)

Falstaff's companions in the tavern are lightly sketched; they will develop as characters in *Henry IV Part II* and in *Henry V*, when joined by Pistol, Doll Tearsheet and Nym. Still, Bardolph and the Hostess can provide a lot of fun on the stage.

Bardolph has been Falstaff's comrade for 32 years, and is his constant butt; he has, however, one comic moment of his own. He and Peto confess that Falstaff's sword was not damaged in battle, but hacked with his own dagger, and that the blood on their clothes came not from any enemy, but from tickling their noses with speargrass.

Shakespeare gives Bardolph a red and purple face (so his blushes can never be seen); it is covered with pimples and boils, which he describes as 'meteors' and 'exhalations' (astrological signs of disaster) portending 'choler', the 'humour' of a fighter. But to the Prince they portend 'collar', the hangman's noose.

Bardolph's face makes Falstaff dub him 'Knight of the Burning Lamp', and reminds Falstaff of hell-fire with purple-robed Dives burning in it, of a will o' the wisp, a ball of wildfire, an everlasting bonfire-light, and much else. Falstaff's jokes about the light from Bardolph's face saving him the expense of a torch, when walking from tavern to tavern, rouses Bardolph to retort, ''Sblood, I would my face were in your belly!' To which Falstaff immediately replies 'God-a-mercy, so should I be sure to be heart-burnt' (III.iii.51).

Mistress Quickly (Quick-lie, suggests Professor Kokeritz) the Hostess, has a very individual, staccato turn of phrase. Her favourite oath prefaces many of her remarks, and she repeats 'O Jesu, my lord, the Prince' (who civilly responds once 'How now, my lady the hostess'). She is devoted to Falstaff, and laughs till she cries at his impersonation of the King, when she draws the audience's attention to his parody of 'one of these harlotry players' (II.iv.404).

Angered by his insistence that his pocket was picked of valuables in her tavern, she gets thoroughly muddled and finally denies that she is a woman:

HOSTESS   God's light! I was never so called in my own house before!

FALSTAFF Go to, I know you well enough.

HOSTESS No, Sir John, you do not know me, Sir John. I know you, Sir John. You owe me money, Sir John, and now you pick a quarrel to beguile me of it. (III.iii.65)

His comic abuse rouses her to vehement denials of everything he says, so that when Falstaff declares that 'a man knows not where to have her', she fiercely libels herself: 'Thou art an unjust man in saying so. Thou or any man knows where to have me, thou knave, thou! (III.iii.132).

When it transpires that it was the Prince who had had Falstaff's pocket picked, Falstaff with supreme impudence dismisses her with 'Hostess, I forgive thee' (III.iii.177) - for his own false suspicions, his unpaid debts for drink and the dozen shirts she has bought for him. Knavery, we see, flourishes in the tavern, and mirrors the knavery in high places.

5.2 STYLE AND LANGUAGE

Blank Verse

Over half of this play is written in blank verse, that is, in lines of ten syllables which have a basic rhythm of *ti-tum*, *ti-tum*, *ti-tum*, *ti-tum*, *ti-tum*. It is the poetic rhythm which is nearest to our everyday speech - many sentimental passages in the novels of Charles Dickens can be written out as blank verse. It is noticeable that the end of Falstaff's prose speech of pleading (II.iv.488-90) falls naturally into three lines of blank verse:

> Banish not him thy Harry's company,
> Banish not him thy Harry's company,
> Banish plump Jack, and banish all the world!

The great advantage of blank verse in the theatre is that it is much easier to learn by heart than prose.

Blank verse can be as complicated as the writer wishes, full of symbols, images and elaborations, but in *Henry IV Part I* Shakespeare writes mainly straightforward, quick-moving lines, suitable for men doing quick political and military manoeuvring. (It is in the tavern that there is time for elaboration, image piled on image in the prose of Falstaff and the Prince. See pages 63-5.)

Hotspur's verse sounds spontaneous; the word order is usually the same as in everyday speech. He has no use for 'mincing poetry' (III.i.132) or 'holiday and lady terms' (I.iii.45). Hotspur says 'I that have not well the gift of tongue' and 'I profess not talking' (V.ii.77, 91). But when he is burning to justify himself and keep his prisoners, and later to vindicate Mortimer, he has two very eloquent passages (I.iii.28-68; 92-111) which seem to burst out naturally, when spoken on stage. It is as if his abundant, overflowing energy found an outlet in an outpouring of speech.

Not every line of blank verse has ten syllables; Shakespeare sometimes indicates how he wishes his lines delivered by inserting pauses. Hotspur's last words (as printed in the First Folio) are:

> No Percy, thou art dust
> And food for —

Hotspur dies during the long pause; then the Prince finishes the sentence:

> For worms, brave Percy, Farewell great heart:

one syllable is missing, between 'Percy' and 'Farewell' – a very effective tiny pause. Unfortunately, modern editors, counting syllables, saw there were only nine and added one: 'Fare *thee* well, great heart!' (V.iv.84).

See page 59 for a detailed analysis of a passage of blank verse (IV.i.97–124).

Prose

Most early Tudor plays were written in rhymed verse, often very crude, and in them only clowns spoke prose. This 'jogtrot' rhyming changed with Christopher Marlowe (1564–93) into blank verse, which was perfected, and made capable of expressing every emotion, by Shakespeare.

In his early writings it is still the clowns who speak prose, but often a very symmetrical and balanced prose, as in *The Comedy of Errors* when Dromio complains of being beaten:

When I am cold	he heats me with beating,
when I am warm	he cools me with beating,
I am waked with it	when I sleep,
raised with it	when I sit,
driven out of doors with it	when I go from home,
welcomed home with it	when I return.

(IV.iv.32)

Before long, more important characters – for instance Shylock in *The Merchant of Venice* – were given prose to speak, but the prose was less than twenty per cent of that play. In *Henry IV Part I* Shakespeare for the first time makes a clear class distinction between prose and poetry speakers, and for the first time nearly forty per cent of the play is in prose.

Prose is spoken in the tavern; verse is spoken at court. Prince Hal, who boasts that he is 'of all humours' (II.iv.93) and that he can 'drink with any tinker in his own language' (II.iv.19), speaks both. In the inn with Falstaff the clown, he answers prose with prose, but when he is left alone (I.ii.200), and when he has to assume his princely rank to get rid of the sheriff

(II.iv.523) or to give orders about the war (III.iii.204), when he speaks with his father at court and on the battlefield, he speaks verse. At Shrewsbury (V.iii) Falstaff as ever speaks prose, but the prince does not, as before, answer him in kind; Hal has cast off the tavern life, and rebukes Falstaff in verse, as a Prince should.

Hotspur speaks a strong, straightforward verse almost all the time. His prose outburst when reading the traitor's letter (II.iii) is full of repetition of words and phrases, and is strongly rhythmical:

> our plot is a good plot as ever was laid;
> our friends true and constant;
> a good plot, good friends and full of expectation;
> an excellent plot, very good friends.

The famous actor William Macready (1793-1873) found that in reading Horspur's letter it was best to keep out 'vehemence and effort'. If the passage is said naturally Shakespeare has so arranged the words that the stresses fall where they are required to emphasise the meaning.

At the meeting of the conspirators (III.i) Hotspur's occasional scraps of prose stand out against the romantic verse of Glendower and the rest. Elizabethan theatregoers must have been far more sensitive to the difference between prose and verse than any modern audience. Shakespeare can assume that they will notice the intrusion of a single line of blank verse. In *As You Like It* Jacques and Rosalind, talking prose, are interrupted by Orlando saying; 'Good day and happiness, dear Rosalind', and Jacques at once retorts, 'Nay, then, God b'w'you, an you talk in blank verse' (IV.i.28). In Marston's play *The Malcontent*, Altofronto speaks verse in his own character, and prose when disguised as Malevole; the stage direction is 'Malevole shifteth his speech'.

In the play-scene (II.iv) Falstaff's prose is a brilliant parody, not only of the heavy manner of the sermoniser, but of the style used by John Lyly in his best-selling novel *Euphues*. This carried to extremes balance and antithesis; it was symmetrical, based on repetition of letters, words, phrases and shapes of sentences, with concealed rhymes and assonance, with allusions to ancient wisdom and to real and fantastic natural history. Lyly might well have written:

> For though the camomile
>   the more it is trodden on,   the faster it grows,
> yet youth
>   the more it is wasted,   the sooner it wears. (II.iv.409)

Another example is:

> I do not speak to thee
>
> | in drink, | but in tears; |
> | not in pleasure, | but in passion; |
> | not in words only, | but in woes also. (II.iv.424) |

The Prince abuses Falstaff:

> | Wherein is he good | but to taste sack and drink it? |
> | Wherein neat and cleanly, | but to carve a capon and eat it? |
> | Wherein cunning, | but in craft? |
> | Wherein crafty, | but in villainy? |
> | Wherein villainous, | but in all things? |
> | Wherein worthy, | but in nothing? (II.iv.464) |

Such an extremely mannered style of speaking emphasises the fact that Falstaff and the Prince are play-acting, but on examination it will be found that much of their seemingly casual conversation is also written in a formal pattern (see page 62).

Wordplay

The Elizabethans enjoyed playing games with words. Learned men were just beginning to write in English instead of Latin, and they were determined to show that they could be just as learned in their native tongue. In school, boys had to learn by heart upwards of a hundred 'figures of speech' (Shakespeare uses over two hundred) and practise inventing examples of them. To take one example, the humble pun (or double meaning), now regarded as suitable only for jokes in Christmas crackers, was a serious literary device; there are about a hundred and fifty puns in *Henry IV Part I*, some fifty of them Falstaff's. A. R. Humphreys, the editor of the Arden edition of the play, is particularly good at noticing and explaining these 'quibbles'.

The pun had four forms, all used lavishly in this play:

Antanaclasis is the repetition of a word, shifting from one meaning to another; for instance, 'crown' is both what a king wears and the top of a man's head (II.iv.386). Again, when the Prince says 'I could have better spared a better man' (V.iv.103), 'better' means first 'more easily' and secondly 'more virtuous'.

Syllepsis is the single use of a word or phrase with two different meanings; for instance, Falstaff is 'in some liking', both 'feels like doing it' and 'is still fat'; soon he will be 'out of heart', both 'not in the mood' and 'in ill-health' (III.iii.5). Again, Falstaff is called 'my sweet creature of bombast' (II.iv.334), 'bombast' meaning both cotton wool used for stuffing, an allusion to his size, and 'elaborate language' such as he often uses. There is a subtle use of this form when Worcester says 'There is no seeming mercy in the king' (V.ii.34), which can mean either that the king does not seem to be merciful, or that the king's mercy is genuine, not 'seeming'.

Paranomasia is the repetition of words almost or quite the same in sound; for instance 'were it not here apparent that thou art heir apparent' (I.ii.60). Other examples are 'pray' and 'prey' (II.i.82), and 'deer' and 'dearer' (V.iv.106).

Asteimus is a word returned by an answerer with an unexpected meaning; for instance, Bardolph says, 'Choler, my lord, if rightly taken', meaning 'Anger, my lord, if properly understood'. But the Prince replies 'No, if rightly taken, halter', meaning, 'No, if justly arrested, a collar, a hangman's noose' (II.iv.331). Again, 'You care not who sees your back,' says Falstaff, 'Call you that backing of your friends?' (II.iv.151), while 'points' means sword-points to Falstaff, but to Poins the laces that held up a man's hose (II.iv.218).

These are only a few examples of the many figures of speech used by Shakespeare, not for their own sake, but to enhance and amplify his meaning, and we can enjoy them without bothering to remember their names.

Images

Shakespeare often makes his meaning more vivid by using images, that is, by comparing one thing with another, in similes and metaphors, or by using words which call up pictures, often moving pictures, to the reader. Sometimes a particular set of images dominate in a play; for instance, in *Romeo and Juliet* many images of flashes of light against darkness typify the brief union of the lovers, so quickly extinguished. But in *Henry IV Part I* there is no predominant group of images, perhaps because the play includes so wide a range of themes, characters and lifestyles.

Images can reflect character. It is noticeable, for instance, that Hotspur's images are often homely and countrified: 'a tired horse, a railing wife. . .a smoky house. . .cheese and garlic in a windmill' (III.i.158); 'a dry wheel grate on the axle-tree' (III.i.130); 'a stubble land at harvest home' (I.iii.34); as befits a 'northern youth' (III.ii.145) brought up far from court. (He has recently been convincingly acted with a Tyneside accent.)

The images in this play come from everything, everywhere. A small sample must suffice. From music, the lover's lute and the drone of a bagpipe (I.ii.80, 81). From the real and imagined qualities of animals, 'a struck fowl or a hurt wild duck' (IV.ii.20), the melancholy hare and the miserable baited bear (I.ii.82, 79), the otter 'neither fish nor flesh' (III.iii.131), and the lion that 'will not touch the true prince' (II.iv.278).

Shakespeare knows about textiles, from the 'flame-coloured taffeta' of the prostitute (I.ii.10) and 'gummed velvet' (II.ii.2), to the difference between coarse 'filthy dowlas' and fine 'holland' linen (III.iii.72, 75). From the Bible, much, including Dives and Lazarus (III.iii.33; IV.ii.25). Much, too, from the kitchen: the huge, soft Falstaff compares himself to a small, shrivelled peppercorn (III.iii.9) and to a 'soused gurnet' (IV.ii.12), and knows how quickly a mackerel becomes stale (II.iv.367). Hal knows how lean joints are 'larded' (II.iii.111) and Hotspur despises a 'dish of skimmed milk' (II.iii.333).

From everyday life there is, too, evidence of the lack of sanitation in the filthy inn (II.i.19) and the filthier Moorditch (I.ii.83). Finally, perhaps from his own boyhood, the schoolboy who plays truant on a sunny day to go blackberrying (II.iv.416).

Shakespeare also uses verbs to make vivid moving pictures. Hotspur says that King Henry, when Bolingbroke, won 'the hearts of all that he did *angle* for', implying that as the fisherman traps the fish with bait, so did Bolingbroke, in order to capture and destroy them.

When the King is describing his early scheming to take away Richard's throne, he does not say 'I was courteous', but 'I *stole* all courtesy from heaven'; not 'I was humble' but 'I *dressed myself* in such humility'; not 'I gained allegiance' but 'I did *pluck* allegiance from men's hearts' – words implying activity, dishonesty, 'dressing-up' and a certain furtiveness (III.ii.50). King Richard II is not described as, say, 'frivolous', but as 'the *skipping* king'; he '*carded* his state'; to 'card' is to adulterate and weaken drink, so Richard diluted his kingship because he 'mingled his royalty with cap'ring fools', and 'capering fools' reinforces the picture of the 'skipping king' (III.ii.60), another lord of misrule.

The word 'horse' occurs some forty times in the play, reminding us of the importance of the horse in those days, both practically and as a status symbol. Whether the business in hand was carrying messages, highway robbery or fighting, a man's life might depend upon his horse. Poins assumes that if he provides masks for the robbers 'you have horses for yourselves' (I.ii.134). But at Gadshill before the robbery Poins has 'removed Falstaff's horse', and Falstaff complains bitterly, 'The rascal hath removed my horse', 'Give me my horse, you rogue, give me my horse' (II.ii.1, 11, 29). Falstaff and company mean to share their booty and 'then to horse' to escape, but the Prince and Poins overcome them and 'merrily to horse' go back to London (II.ii.101, 107).

Shakespeare uses horses to give a sense of haste and urgency. The King's messenger 'did take horse' (I.i.60); Sir Walter Blunt is 'new-lighted from his horse' (I.i.63); Glendower will 'to horse immediately' (III.i.266).

Horsemanship is also a measure of valour: Falstaff has heard that Douglas can run 'a-horseback up a hill perpendicular'. The Prince goes one better: 'He that rides at high speed, and with his pistol kills a sparrow flying.' 'You have hit it,' says Falstaff, but the Prince deflates Douglas:

'So did he never the sparrow' (II.iv.350). When war summons them away from Eastcheap, Falstaff the 'horseback breaker' (II.iv.268), partly as an unkind joke, but also as indicating his rank, is only given 'a charge of foot' soldiers, and says regretfully, 'I would it had been of horse' (III.iii.193). We know that to him 'eight yards of uneven ground is three score and ten miles afoot' (II.ii.25).

Hotspur, as his name shows, is most at home 'a-horseback' (II.iii.102); 'that roan shall be my throne' (II.iii.71); his horse 'carries [him] away' (II.iii.76) from his protesting wife, and indeed seems to be of more importance to him, since he ignores her while making sure that it is his favourite 'roan' horse, about which the Prince jests (II.iv.108). Vernon's praise of the Prince's 'noble horsemanship' is the last straw to Hotspur, and makes him determined to encounter the Prince 'hot horse to horse', having no doubt of his own victory (IV.i.107, 122). But we have seen the Prince leaving the tavern behind as he calls 'to horse, to horse' and uttering in his turn a challenge:

> The land is burning, Percy stands on high,
> And either we or they must lower lie. (III.iii.204, 209).

6 ANALYSIS OF SPECIMEN PASSAGES

6.1 BLANK VERSE

Hotspur, preparing for battle, asks where the 'nimble-footed madcap Prince of Wales and his comrades' are to be found. Let us look closely at Vernon's enthusiastic description of the Prince, and Hotspur's furious reply. Vernon begins:

>   All furnished, all in arms;
> All plumed like estridges that with the wind
> Bated like eagles having lately bathed;
> Glittering in golden coats like images;
> As full of spirit as the month of May
> And gorgeous as the sun at midsummer;
> Wanton as youthful goats, wild as young bulls.
> I saw young Harry with his beaver on,
> His cushes on his thighs, gallantly armed,
> Rise from the ground like feathered Mercury,
> And vaulted with such ease into his seat
> As if an angel dropped down from the clouds
> To turn and wind a fiery Pegasus
> And witch the world with noble horsemanship.

> HOTSPUR   No more, no more! Worse than the sun in March,
> This praise doth nourish agues. Let them come.
> They come like sacrifices in their trim,
> And to the fire-eyed maid of smoky war
> All hot and bleeding will we offer them.
> The mailèd Mars shall on his altar sit
> Up to the ears in blood. I am on fire
> To hear this rich reprisal is so nigh,

> And yet not ours! Come, let me taste my horse,
> Who is to bear me like a thunderbolt
> Against the bosom of the Prince of Wales.
> Harry to Harry shall, hot horse to horse,
> Meet, and ne'er part till one drop down a corse.
> O that Glendower were come!   (IV.i.97-124)

Vernon's three times repeated 'all' implies all together, in unity, as opposed to the divided rebels. The plumes in the knights' helmets waved in the wind like ostriches that 'bated' [beat their wings]. 'Estridge' can also mean 'goshawk', a large falcon, and 'bated' can suggest 'baited' or refreshed, like newly-bathed eagles shaking the water from their great wings. The passage is full of symbols of royalty: as the king was the first of men, so eagle, gold and sun were respectively first of birds, metals and planets:

> Glittering in golden coats like images;
> As full of spirit as the month of May
> And gorgeous as the sun at midsummer;
> Wanton as youthful goats, wild as young bulls. (IV.i.100)

Images in golden coats recall the gilded effigies of nobles on medieval tombs (as in the Beauchamp Chapel at Warwick, only eight miles from Stratford) and 'coats' are both armour, coats of mail, and sleeveless tunics painted with heraldic coats of arms, worn to distinguish individuals when the helmet was closed over the face (as the king at Shrewsbury had 'many marching in his coats' (V.iii.25)). The first of May was the traditional annual festival of youth and love; the Prince and his companions have the energy and freshness of May, as well as the glory of the sun at its highest point in June. They have the exuberance of '*youthful* goats' or '*young* bulls', the repetition emphasising their youth, lustiness and strength.

> I saw young Harry with his beaver on,
> His cushes on his thighs, gallantly armed,
> Rise from the ground like feathered Mercury,
> And vaulted with such ease into his seat
> As if an angel dropped down from the clouds
> To turn and wind a fiery Pegasus
> And witch the world with noble horsemanship. (IV.i.104)

The Prince was fully armed, wearing his beaver (the face-guard on his helmet) and his cushes [cuisses], his thigh armour. Despite this weight he vaulted to his horse's back as easily as pagan Mercury (the messenger of the gods, who flew with winged sandals), or a Christian angel, might alight – thus showing extraordinary strength and agility, for knights in full armour usually had to be hoisted into their saddles. Even the horse is transformed into 'fiery Pegasus', the winged horse of Greek myths, and is managed so skilfully that everyone is bewitched. The whole description is written in easy, natural-sounding lines, as if spoken spontaneously.

At this account of the Prince, Hotspur is astounded, and furious. He stops Vernon:

> No more, no more! Worse than the sun in March,
> This praise doth nourish agues. (IV.i.111)

The weak sun in March was thought strong enough to excite the blood and stir up 'humours' in it, but not strong enough to expel them. The victim would shiver with fever, as this praise of the Prince might make the rebels shiver with fear. But as ever Hotspur is ready to fight anyone, anywhere:

> Let them come.
> They come like sacrifices in their trim,
> And to the fire-eyed maid of smoky war
> All hot and bleeding will we offer them.
> The mailèd Mars shall on his altar sit
> Up to the ears in blood.   (IV.i.112)

Instead of the newly-bathed, open-air freshness, the green and gold of May and June, and the vitality of Vernon's description, Hotspur pictures a smoky interior, hot, stuffy and awash with blood. The gorgeous garments Vernon described seem to Hotspur like the garlands put on beasts before sacrificial slaughter, 'their trim'. Hotspur as priest will sacrifice the Prince and his comrades, newly slain, to Mars and Bellona, god and goddess of war.

> I am on fire
> To hear this rich reprisal is so nigh
> And yet not ours! Come let me taste my horse,
> Who is to bear me like a thunderbolt
> Against the bosom of the Prince of Wales.
> Harry to Harry shall, hot horse to horse,
> Meet, and ne'er part till one drop down a corse. (IV.i.117)

As ever, Hotspur is 'on fire to go' (III.i.264) and as before calls for his horse, his 'throne' (II.iii.71), to put him on equal terms with the Prince. In contrast to Vernon's light, soaring, fresh images, Hotspur's speech is extraordinarily heated, vivid, violent and destructive – 'fire-eyed', 'hot and bleeding', 'on fire', 'thunderbolt', 'hot horse' – and he ends the outburst with a final rhymed couplet for emphasis. Very effectively, Shakespeare adds a last line in a totally different tone: 'O that Glendower were come!' as Hotspur sobers and realises the odds against the rebels.

There are three contemporary passages which seem closely related to this description of the Prince; if only one existed it would be cited as a 'source' - Shakespeare may have read any or all of them. First, a description in Thomas Nashe's *The Unfortunate Traveller*, of the Earl of Surrey riding to a tournament on a horse 'bolstered out' in the 'shape of an Estrich', with quivering wings, like Pegasus. Next, Spenser's Red Cross Knight, in *The Faerie Queene*, rises to battle from the Well of Life, new-born, 'as Eagle, fresh out of the Ocean wave'. Lastly, Chapman's description of Sir Walter Ralegh going off to Guiana; the expressions 'his bating colours', 'a wind as forward as their spirits' and 'valour estrich-like' occur within eleven lines. All three can be found in the Arden edition of *Henry IV Part I*, and the first two in the Cambridge edition. It is obvious that one should be very wary of claiming to have discovered one of Shakespeare's 'sources'.

6.2 PROSE

FALSTAFF   Now, Hal, what time of day is it, lad?

PRINCE   Thou art so fat-witted with drinking of old sack, and unbuttoning thee after supper, and sleeping upon benches after noon, that thou hast forgotten to demand that truly which thou wouldst truly know. What a devil hast thou to do with the time of the day? Unless hours were cups of sack, and minutes capons, and clocks the tongues of bawds, and dials the signs of leaping houses, and the blessed sun himself a fair hot wench in flame-coloured taffeta, I see no reason why thou shouldst be so superfluous to demand the time of the day.

FALSTAFF   Indeed you come near me now, Hal; for we that take purses go by the moon and the seven stars, and not 'by Phoebus, he, that wand.ring knight so fair'. And I prithee, sweet wag, when thou art a king, as, God save thy Grace - Majesty I should say, for grace thou wilt have none -

PRINCE   What, none?

FALSTAFF   No, by my troth; not so much as will serve to be prologue to an egg and butter.

PRINCE   Well, how then? Come, roundly, roundly.

FALSTAFF   Marry, then, sweet wag, when thou art king, let not us that are squires of the night's body be called thieves of the day's beauty. Let us be Diana's foresters, gentlemen of the shade, minions of the moon; and let men say we be men of good government, being governed, as the sea is, by our noble and chaste mistress the moon, under whose countenance we steal.

PRINCE Thou sayest well, and it holds well too; for the fortune of us that are the moon's men doth ebb and flow like the sea, being governed as the sea is by the moon. As, for proof now: a purse of gold most resolutely snatched on Monday night and most dissolutely spent on Tuesday morning; got with swearing 'Lay by,' and spent with crying 'Bring in'; now in as low an ebb as the foot of the ladder, and by and by in as high a flow as the ridge of the gallows. (I.ii.1-40)

After the verse spoken at court in the first scene in the play it must have been a surprise for the audience to hear at the opening of the second scene Falstaff's casual question and the Prince's response, in prose. Falstaff speaks as to an equal, 'Now, Hal, what time of day is it, lad?' And the Prince replies in a prose which when spoken sounds spontaneous and natural, but when investigated is seen to be carefully arranged with balanced phrases, clauses and sentences.

Thou art so fat-witted   with drinking of old sack [wine],
                               and unbuttoning thee after supper,
                               and sleeping upon benches after noon,
That thou hast forgotten to demand that truly
                               which thou wouldst truly know.
What a devil hast thou to do with the time of the day?
Unless hours   were   cups of sack,
and minutes   capons,
and clocks   the tongues of bawds,
and dials   the signs of leaping houses,
and the blessed sun himself a fair hot wench in flame-coloured taffeta
I see no reason why thou shouldst be so superfluous [needlessly
    inquisitive *and* self-indulgent] to demand the time of the day. (2)

Falstaff is 'Fat-witted' from indulging in three of the seven deadly sins - gluttony, sloth and lechery - thus he has 'Forgotten' to think what he is saying. Why should he need to know the time? 'Hours', 'minutes', 'clocks', 'dials' and the ultimate time-marker, the 'sun', are for honest working citizens. For Falstaff they are replaced by 'cups of sack' and 'capons' for feasting, 'bawds', brothels and prostitutes for nightly revels. The question which ends the first part of the speech is answered in the final sentence. Prostitutes wore red petticoats; notice that instead of 'red' or 'scarlet' the '*hot*' wench' wears a '*flame-coloured*' petticoat to emphasise the heat of lust.

This speech not only places Falstaff in a world of idle gorging of food and drink, sleeping by day and frequenting prostitutes by night, it also establishes the Prince's mocking, almost bullying, but amused, attitude to Falstaff.

FALSTAFF Indeed you come near me now, Hal; for we that take
purses go by the moon and the seven stars, and not by
'Phoebus, he, that wand'ring knight so fair'. And I
prithee, sweet wag, when thou art a king, as, God save
thy Grace - Majesty I should say, for grace thou wilt
have none -

PRINCE What, none?

FALSTAFF No, by my troth; not so much as will serve to be prologue to an egg and butter.

PRINCE Well, how then? Come, roundly, roundly. (13)

Falstaff's reply exemplifies the way he gets out of difficulties by appearing
to agree but evading the point of the accusation. He takes 'day' to be the
opposite to night, and admits that highway robbery, by night, is his trade.
He calls the Prince 'sweet wag' [dear lad], and mentions what is always in
his mind, the time 'when thou art king' - confirming the audience's guess
that 'Hal' is indeed the Prince of Wales. Falstaff goes on, punning on
'grace', which is in turn a royal title, as it were 'your Majesty', spiritual
'grace' from God, 'grace' in the sense of cultivated and refined behaviour,
and 'grace' said before meals. Falstaff may be hinting that the Prince has
little claim to a royal title, since his father seized the throne by force, and
certainly only a little 'grace' would suffice for so slight a meal as an egg
and butter.

The Prince puns in reply; 'roundly, roundly' not only means 'talk
plainly', but obviously gives the actor a chance to mock Falstaff's great
belly.

FALSTAFF Marry, then, sweet wag, when thou art king, let not us
that are squires of the night's body be called thieves of
the day's beauty. Let us be Diana's foresters, gentlemen
of the shade, minions of the moon; and let men say we
be men of good government, being governed, as the sea
is, by our noble and chaste mistress the moon, under
whose countenance we steal.

PRINCE Thou sayest well, and it holds well too; for the fortune
of us that are the moon's men doth ebb and flow like
the sea, being governed as the sea is by the moon. As, for
proof now; a purse of gold must resolutely snatched on
Monday night and most dissolutely spent on Tuesday
morning; got with swearing 'Lay by', and spent with
crying 'Bring in'; now in as low an ebb as the foot of the
ladder, and by and by in as high a flow as the ridge of
the gallows. (23)

Falstaff continues his daydream of Hal as king, still fantasising in a flurry of puns, balancing 'squires of the night's body' against 'thieves of the day's beauty'. Squires attended a *knight's* body, *bawdy* work went on at night, at night they gathered *booty* to match 'the day's beauty'. A host of links can be found. Falstaff idealises their trade: the sun was Phoebus; the moon Diana, the goddess huntress; they are her foresters, her darlings and servants, as they hunt for purses 'under [her] countenance', that is both 'with her approval' and 'under the moon's face', and so they 'steal' – both 'rob' and 'go stealthily'. Almost every phrase has two meanings: 'men of good government' 'have a good ruler' – Diana – and 'are well-behaved', one of Falstaff's gross misstatements.

The Prince matches this witty talk, but turns serious. He accepts Falstaff's fantasy, but shows it ending in disaster. The moon governs the sea, which ebbs and flows; so, too, will the fortunes of the moon's men. Hal deftly lists three comparisons: the *resolute* snatching but *dissolute* spending of a purse; the halting of travellers with swearing, 'Lay by', and spending with crying, 'Bring in' [drink] ; the ebb which sets a highwayman at the foot of the gallows ladder which he must climb, as if swept by high tide, to be hanged.

In forty lines of prose Shakespeare has exhibited his skill with words, established two major characters, indicated their relationship, and introduced the idea that robbers will eventually hang – a dread to which Falstaff continually returns.

7 THE PLAY

ON THE STAGE

7.1 STAGE HISTORY

It is important to remember that Shakespeare wrote *plays*; not poems to
be read silently in the study, nor passages to be prepared for examinations,
but plays to be acted, to he heard, to be spoken or shouted or whispered
to noisy audiences, whose cracking of nuts must have been as infuriating
as today's rustling of chocolate wrappers.

So it is important to act as much of the play as possible, or at least to
read it aloud with friends, 'hamming it up' to make up for the lack of action.

Some critics forget that they are talking about a play. One is scornful
about the 'comic touches, such as they are' and 'such comedy as exists' at
the beginning of II.i. But in the theatre the grumbling carters invariably
cause laughter - probably because theirs is the sort of conversation to be
heard in any hotel car park today.

Henry IV Part I was probably acted first in 1597 or 1598, but the first
performance for which there is evidence was ordered by the Lord
Chamberlain in 1600 to entertain the Flemish Ambassador. Two plays,
called *The Hotspur* and *Sir John Falstaff* were acted at the wedding of the
Princess Elizabeth in 1613, and were probably Parts I and II of *Henry IV*.
The first Falstaff we know of is John Lowin (1576-1659) who joined the
King's Company in 1603 and whose Falstaff was greeted with 'mighty
applause'.

The Puritans were determined to prevent play-acting, and in 1642
Parliament ordered all the theatres to close. Actors sometimes tried to
perform, but in 1648 the Lord Mayor was authorised to pull the theatres
down and to flog the actors. Still, 'drolls', extracts from complete plays,
were sometimes surreptitiously acted, and one of these, *The Bouncing
Knight*, consisted of the tavern scenes from *Henry IV*.

When King Charles II was restored to the throne in 1660, Thomas
Killigrew (1612-83) collected a company of pre-Civil War actors, and

performed *Henry IV Part I* at the Red Bull in Clerkenwell. In August 1660 he was licensed to open a new theatre, and put on the same play, and in 1663 he built the first theatre on the spot where the Theatre Royal, Drury Lane, now stands. The diarist Samuel Pepys (1633-1703) saw *Henry IV Part I* no fewer than four times between 1660 and 1667, and enjoyed most 'Falstaff's speech about "What is honour?"'.

Thomas Betterton (1635?-1710), the leading actor of this period, played Hotspur in 1682, and though he was forty-seven it was said to be one of his 'most capital exhibitions', with 'fierce and flashing fire'. In 1699 he changed to Falstaff, and drew 'better audiences than in any new play', continuing in the part for eight years. The play was heavily cut, but no extra speeches were added.

Between 1704 and 1750 *Henry IV Part I* was acted in London every single year - some 220 performances in all. James Quin (1693-1766) played Hotspur in 1718-19, Henry IV in 1720-21, and from 1722 till his retirement in 1751 he played Falstaff, with a superior air and 'supercilious brow'. David Garrick, who dominated the London theatre from 1741 to 1776, joined Quin in 1746 as Hotspur, but failed to get his usual 'thunder of applause', and only played the part five times. To read that 'his dress as Hotspur was objected to: a laced frock and a Ramalie wig were thought too insignificant for the character', reminds us that contemporary dress was still being worn on the stage, whatever the period of the play. A laced frock was a long coat with full skirts, decorated with gold lace, and a Ramalie wig had a long plait behind, with a bow at top and bottom - curious attire indeed for Hotspur.

Not until 1824 was there an attempt to use appropriate historical costumes. Then Charles Kemble (1775-1854) revived *Henry IV Part I* 'in the precise habit of the period. . .executed from. . .Monumental Effigies, Painted Glass and Illuminated Manuscripts'. Elaborate pictorial backcloths showed 'Inn yard at Rochester, with the Castle - Night', 'Shrewsbury from the Field of Battle', and so on.

Many famous players attempted to act Falstaff, including *Mrs* Webb (d.1793) and Stephen Kemble (1758-1822) who was so fat he played Falstaff without padding. Falstaff was also the subject of the first public lecture given on Shakespeare, by William Kendrick in 1774, and of the first criticism that treated one of Shakespeare's characters as if he was a living person: Maurice Morgann's *Essay on . . . Sir John Falstaff* (1777) which staunchly maintained that he was not a coward.

No play by Shakespeare was ever performed with his entire text between 1660 and 1880. They were usually much shortened (Henry IV's speeches, for instance, were thought 'much too long') but often there were also additional speeches and characters. *King Lear*, for instance, omitted the Fool, and had a happy ending with Cordelia marrying Edgar, for some 150 years. Towards the end of the eighteenth century the play scene in the tavern was often omitted from *Henry IV Part I* because one editor thought it 'vastly too long' and 'an incumbrance to the acting' and another called it 'dreadfully tedious in representation'. As actresses became more popular, this play was put on less often, because of the 'want of ladies' and also of 'matter to interest the female auditors'. Charles Lamb the essayist (1775–1834) thought the part of Falstaff 'incompatible with stage representation'.

From the Restoration in 1660 till 1843 the only two theatres in London licensed to produce straight plays were Drury Lane and Covent Garden. This monopoly was ended in 1843 and other theatres could put on Shakespeare. Samuel Phelps (1804–78) at Sadler's Wells Theatre between 1844 and 1862 'made Shakespeare pay'; he put on all but six of Shakespeare's plays, and was an outstanding Falstaff himself.

In 1864, to celebrate the tercentenary of Shakespeare's birth, a magnificent revival of *Henry IV Part I* was staged, with an extra part for 'Lady Glendwyer', and including III.i for the first time since the seventeenth century. There were thirteen pictorial scenes, from 'The King's Antechamber' to 'Field of Battle near Shrewsbury (Sunset)'. At the end 'numerous combattants. . .in bright armour. . .filled the stage with their glittering figures. . .all in vivid action and stirring combat'. The audience received this with 'repeated plaudits'. Doubtless it was magnificent, but was it Shakespeare?

These tremendously elaborate stage sets took so long to erect and dismantle that the text of the plays had to be heavily cut. But in 1881 William Poel (1852–1934) began to present the whole text of Shakespeare's plays, acted on a simple stage in front of plain curtains. He showed that this sort of production was perfectly intelligible, and that Shakespeare had, whenever necessary, put clues about time and place into the text of the plays. For instance, ''Charles' Wain is over the new chimney' (II.i.2) or 'How bloodily the sun begins to peer' (V.i.1).

There were no painted backclothes on the Elizabethan public stage. Push out a throne, and the stage becomes a palace; benches at a table covered with bottles and mugs transform the stage to an inn. The illusion was in the actors – a man wearing a crown was clearly a king, and it will be noticed that the characters are named as they are to speak: 'my gentle cousin Westmoreland' (I.i.31), 'here is. . .Sir Walter Blunt'(I.i.62), 'Now, Hal' (I.ii.1), 'Poins' (I.ii.112). When place is unimportant, it is not mentioned; when necessary (for instance in II.i) it is.

In the twentieth century there have been frequent performances of the histories, in sequence and individually, particularly by the Royal Shakespeare Company at Stratford. In 1964 John Barton arranged the three parts of *Henry VI* as two plays 'Henry VI' and 'Edward IV' and these were played as a complete cycle with the other five English histories, to great effect and applause.

7.2 STRUCTURE OF THE PLAY

This play includes both high and low life, and there are three separate worlds: of the court, the tavern and the rebels. Each has a central figure: the King, Falstaff and Hotspur respectively. Prince Hal inhabits both court and tavern, and at Shrewsbury enters the world of the rebels and defeats Hotspur. At the same time he abandons the tavern world, for at the moment when the Prince kills Hotspur, Douglas 'kills' Falstaff - the audience think that Falstaff is dead. The original stage direction is 'Enter Douglas: he fights with Falstaff, who falls as if he were dead. The Prince killeth Percy'.

It is odd how parts of the Prince's speech to the dead Hotspur apply in a different sense to Falstaff, too:

> When that this body did contain a spirit
> A kingdom for it was too small a bound. . .
> . . .so stout a gentleman. . .   (V.iv.88)

And when the Prince turns to Falstaff's body and says that he will have it 'embowelled' - so that it can be preserved for burial at home - this would in another sense have been the appropriate punishment for the rebel Percy, since traitors were hanged, drawn and quartered - that is, strangled and then disembowelled.

Hotspur's part is finished; his rivalry and example have turned the Prince into a soldier. Falstaff, however, is like Punch in the traditional *Punch and Judy* puppet show, always being snubbed and knocked down, but always bouncing back again. Falstaff must survive, still embodying disorder and riot, in *Henry IV Part II*, which will show the Prince choosing between order and disorder, law and riot, in civil life.

Sir John Falstaff is no mere cardboard figure from a morality play; he is a great comic creation who is a many-sided character, and the comic scenes in which he appears are absolutely essential to the play. Shakespeare alternates and links the comic and serious events of the play, so that Falstaff's words and behaviour continually mimic the serious action. Again and again incidents and speeches mirror and parody each other, most notably perhaps when the fatal duel between Hal and Hotspur is mimicked on the other side of the stage by the mock contest between the Douglas and Falstaff.

At Gadshill Falstaff robs the travellers, but is robbed in his turn by the Prince and Poins. King Henry has stolen Richard's throne, but his old allies the Percys are now trying to rob him of his spoils. 'A plague upon it', says Falstaff, 'when thieves cannot be true one to another' (II.ii.27). But there is no honour among thieves, or, for that matter, among rebels. Falstaff and his men are deserted at the moment of action by the Prince and Poins;

Hotspur is deserted by the Lord who withdraws his support, and later even by his father Northumberland and Glendower.

When we meet the King first he is planning a crusade; the Prince is planning a highway robbery, 'Where shall we take a purse tomorrow, Jack?' (I.ii.96). We see the Prince preparing to play a practical joke on his tavern companions (II.i) while Hotspur is off to fight in earnest (II.iii). Gadshill boasts of his powerful friends who will 'make all whole' if necessary (II.i.70); Hotspur boasts of his friends, 'good friends. . .very good friends' (II.iii.18); both are let down.

Falstaff is used as a foil for Hotspur, and not only in the matter of 'honour' (see p. 36). Hotspur's 'easy leap' to the pale-faced moon' seems slightly ridiculous contrasted with Falstaff's practical and plaintive, 'Have you any levers to lift me up again, being down?' (II.ii.34). Hotspur complains of the cowardly lord who will not fight with them (II.iii.15); in comes Falstaff, repeating, 'A plague on all cowards' (II.iv.115, 118, 135). Is Hotspur's romantic account of Glendower's fight with Mortimer (I.iii.93-111) just as exaggerated in its own way as Falstaff's story of his struggle with the men in buckram? (II.iv.167-228).

Immediately after Vernon's description of the Prince, ready for war, fully armed and on horseback, 'glittering', 'golden', 'gorgeous' (IV.i.100), we are told of Falstaff's tattered scarecrows, ragged slaves, pitiful rascals, compelled to fight in a quarrel they know nothing about; only three of the hundred and fifty will survive, and they will be maimed (IV.ii; V.iii). In Act V Falstaff has to face the fact that this is real, not mock, fighting. He may be killed. The Percys are not men in buckram to be slain with talking. And the fates of Falstaff and Hotspur each emphasise the futility of war: Hotspur dies honourably, but his 'sport' has caused many other deaths. Falstaff survives, but so dishonourably as to change our feelings about him.

The interview between the King and Hal in III.ii has already been rehearsed twice, in the tavern, by Hal and Falstaff, parodying the relationship of the King and his heir. Play-acting in the tavern, Falstaff does not sustain his part either as King or Prince; he uses the occasion to make first a joking, then a passionate, appeal for the Prince's continued friendship (II.iv.431-40, 480-90). The Prince brutally abuses him, going far beyond a joke: 'that trunk of humours. . .that huge bombard of sack, that stuffed cloak-bag of guts. . .that reverend vice, that grey iniquity, that father ruffian. . .that villainous abominable misleader of youth, Falstaff, that old white-bearded Satan' (459, 472). And the answer to Falstaff's impassioned plea to the pretence king: 'Banish not him thy Harry's company' (488) is uncompromising, covering both present and future: 'I do. I will' (491).

When the real interview between King and Prince follows, a similar appeal for Hal's loyalty is made, and we know already what the answer will be, though perhaps it is a surprise to hear Hal adopt the values of

Hotspur (much as it pleases his father). The Prince says that he will

> . . .in the closing of some glorious day
> Be bold to tell you that I am your son,
> When I will wear a garment all of blood
> And stain my favours in a bloody mask
> Which, washed away, shall scour my shame with it. (III.ii.133)

A mere fifty lines later Falstaff too 'repents' – for the moment – 'Well, I'll repent, and that suddenly, while I am in some liking. I shall be out of heart shortly, and then I shall have no strength to repent' (III.iii.5). The Prince's repentance will be more lasting.

Apart from the play-acting in the tavern, there is a great deal of role-playing throughout. Henry IV tells Hal that a king must be politic; he must create an image of himself that appeals to the public – as he himself did when Henry Bolingbroke. Hal's whole lifestyle in the tavern is a deliberate assumption of a temporary role. At Gadshill the prince and Poins disguise themselves for a jest; at Shrewsbury several people disguise themselves as the King, to save his life in earnest.

7.3 FALSTAFF AS VICE

It is traditional in England to insert comic scenes into the most serious plays. In the earliest biblical 'mystery' plays Mrs Noah is carried kicking and screaming into the Ark, and the torturers jest about the weight as they raise Christ's cross. Sometimes the comic moments reflect the main plot: Mak the shepherd steals a sheep, hides it in a baby's cradle, is discovered and is tossed in a blanket, before his fellows go off to Bethlehem to see Christ, the Lamb of God, in his manger cradle.

In early Tudor plays there are the same patterns; the serious action is interrupted by irrelevant scenes of crude fooling, fighting between Huf, Ruf and Snuf, or Hob and Lob blinding a man with lather from a chamber-pot and then stealing his purse. A character known as the 'Vice', related to the devils of the mystery plays, appears in the comic scenes making mischief, and in the tragic scenes stirring up serious trouble.

The Elizabethans were accustomed to 'moralities' in which almost all of the characters were personifications; 'Everyman' or 'Mankind' was tempted by such sins as Avarice, Gluttony and Lechery, but could be rescued by Good Deeds or an Angel. 'Interludes' were short, and often comic, they borrowed from the moralities abstract sins, but turned them into people and exhibited their ridiculous side – the 'Vice' might be Vanity or Riot – wanton wasteful living and debauchery.

In the popular interlude *Youth* (published in several editions by 1562) a young man simply entitled 'Youth' scorns Charity (Love), and instead chooses to live with Riot (who is 'full of jollity'), Pride and Lechery. Riot is a highway robber who escapes from the hangman, steals a purse, and takes Youth (who is 'the heir of my father's land') to a tavern. At the end, despite Riot's pleading: 'I am sure thou wilt not forsake me', the reformed Youth declares 'I forsake you also and will not have with you to do'.

Professor Arthur Quiller-Couch suggests that *Henry IV Part I* can be seen as a morality play entitled *The Contention between Virtue and Vice for the Soul of a Prince* – in which, of course, Falstaff is the Vice. There are hints of this in the text of the play.

The conventional Vice, embodying Idleness, Gluttony and Lechery, was equipped with a 'dagger of lath', a thin sliver of wood with which he would try to fight, or to pare the devil's claws. Falstaff tells the Prince that he will 'beat thee out of thy kingdom with a dagger of lath' (II.iv.139). The Prince refers to Falstaff as 'a devil. . .in the likeness of an old fat man', 'that reverend vice. . .that grey iniquity. . .that vanity in years. . .that villainous abominable misleader of youth' (II.iv.139, 456, 463, 472). 'Riot' and 'Vanity' are appropriate nicknames for Falstaff, who wishes to abolish all authority, scorns 'old father antic the law' (I.ii.64) and lives 'out of all order, out of all compass' (III.iii.21).

7.4 HAL AND HOTSPUR

Thomas Hardy wrote a poem on the loss of the liner *Titanic*, called *The Convergence of the Twain (1914)*. It tells how from the ship's first building and the birth of the iceberg they slowly but inevitably draw together, until finally they meet, disastrously. This is not unlike the story of the Prince and Hotspur.

At the beginning of the play the Prince of Wales and Hotspur are far apart in place and in esteem. They are introduced together in the first scene by the King's bitter comparison of his wastrel son with Hotspur, who is 'the theme of honour's tongue', 'sweet fortune's minion' (I.i.80), and they are shown to us subsequently in alternate scenes. Gradually they approach each other, the Prince improving and Hotspur growing less attractive, until finally they meet on the battlefield 'Harry to Harry,. . . and ne'er part till one drop down a corse' (IV.i.122).

Our first sight of the Prince catches him lazing in the tavern, while valiant Hotspur, the hero of a battle, is shown defending his behaviour with force and wit (I.iii.28–68), but afterwards losing his temper like a thwarted child. In Act II Hotspur goes off to fight, and in contrast the Prince goes off to indulge in highway robbery, and returns to the tavern mocking Hotspur; he is truly 'Not yet of Percy's mind' (II.iv.102).

But Hotspur, when he meets the rebel leaders in Wales, is shown as rude, boorish, unable to agree with his fellow conspirators. The King sends for Hal, and by comparing him with Hotspur stings the Prince into boasting that he will one day defeat this 'northern youth' and make him 'render every glory up' (III.ii.145, 150).

Hotspur grows ever more rash; a momentary softening, when he is willing to consider peace, vanishes when his uncle betrays both King and rebels by concealing the King's offer of pardon. Meanwhile we hear a dazzling account of the Prince as a warrior, 'gallantly armed' (IV.i.105). (See page 59.)

In the last act the reversal is complete; the Prince saves his father's life and meets Hotspur in single combat. Hal carries out his promise to 'redeem all [his ill deeds] on Percy's head', and to take 'every honour sitting on his helm' (III.ii.132, 142), while the dying Hotspur laments the loss of his 'proud titles' (V.iv.78). The Prince declared before the fight that 'Percy stands on high, and either we or they must lower lie' (III.iii.209). The rivalry ends with the Prince standing triumphantly yet sadly over the fallen Hotspur.

8 CRITICAL RECEPTION

Samples of the vast amount of criticism which has been written about *Henry IV Part I* are given here. The books written by these critics are listed as 'Further Reading' on page 82.

An excellent book for both general reader and specialist, covering all aspects of Shakespeare's English histories, is M. M. Reese's *The Cease of Majesty*; comprehensive and clearly written, it relates the plays to the political thought of Shakespeare's period.

E. M. W. Tillyard's account is perhaps over-simplified, but it gives a real sense of the whole sweep of the English histories as a meaningful sequence, and of the immense variety of the life shown in them. He emphasises the Elizabethan view that war and rebellion were 'unnatural' aberrations in what should be an ordered world. Incidentally, he defends Hal from attacks by other critics.

Lily B. Campbell gives a scholarly account of the historical background, particularly as regards Elizabethan views on rebellion, and emphasises that Elizabethans expected the study of history to illumine the present.

Many critics have concentrated on Falstaff. Maurice Morgann's enthusiastic essay in 1777 stoutly maintained, in a lengthy argument, that he was not a coward. Dr Samuel Johnson brought his massive common sense to bear in 1765, and though he praised Falstaff as 'unimitated, unimitable' saw that he was 'a character loaded with faults', ' compound of sense and vice', who yet had 'the most pleasing of all qualities, perpetual gaiety'.

A. C. Bradley writes with some pleasure of Falstaff's freedom from ordinary scruples: 'he is the enemy of everything respectable and moral. . . they are all to him absurd'. Bradley also considers Hal and notes his likeness to what his father was when still merely Henry Bolingbroke (in *Richard II*).

J. Palmer reminds us that however corrupt Falstaff may be, he is no more corrupt than King or rebels - each of them is out for what he can get, by any manner of means.

H. B. Charlton, another of Falstaff's admirers, praises his 'unslakeable thirst for life' and the way in which he meets with every kind of disaster, but always survives. Charlton suggests that the true hero of the history plays is simply England.

J. Dover Wilson has been perhaps the most influential critic of *Henry IV Part I*. He has devoted a whole book to *The Fortunes of Falstaff*, tracing his possible origins in early Tudor drama, in miracle play, morality and interlude, and analysing in great detail his character and behaviour. Today it is often forgotten that the military virtues, through military, are also virtues, and Dover Wilson asks the reader to recognise the Elizabethan belief in 'absolute monarchy, the feudal system, the military virtues', which Hal embodies. He points out how Hal's relations with his father, Falstaff and Hotspur are part of his education as a prince; and he admires Hal's devotion to duty, in *Henry IV Part II* and *Henry V*.

C. L. Barber also looks backwards for Falstaff's predecessors and sees him as Lord of Misrule, who presided over the Feast of Fools at Christmas time.

W. H. Auden takes an extreme view. To him Falstaff is the embodiment of supernatural 'charity'; he loves everyone, so all his faults must be ignored or at least forgiven. Yet Auden rightly observes that 'sober reflection in the study may tell us that Falstaff is not, after all, a very admirable person, but Falstaff on the stage gives us no time for sober reflection'.

At the other extreme, G. B. Shaw, delighting in shocking his readers, wrote that Hal was 'a combination of conventional propriety and brute masterfulness in his public capacity, with a low-lived blackguardism in his private tastes'.

D. Traversi goes through *Henry IV Part I* scene by scene, and has real insights, despite treating the work as reading matter, and not as a play.

So many critics, so many opinions. Much the best thing to do is to see the play acted, if possible, and/or to act it yourself, and read it closely, and then make up your own mind about Falstaff and Hal and Hotspur.

REVISION QUESTIONS

1. 'Divided sympathy is characteristic of Shakespeare's history plays.' How are your sympathies divided in *Henry IV Part I*?

2. Discuss some of the meanings of the word 'honour' as illustrated in *Henry IV Part I*.

3. What justification, if any, is there for regarding *Henry IV Part I* as a morality play about the education of a prince?

4. What is (i) the apparent and (ii) the real relationship between the Prince and Falstaff?

5. Choose three of the following, and describe how they affect our opinion of major characters: Bardolph, Glendower, Sir Richard Vernon, Lady Percy, Worcester, the Hostess.

6. The play-acting in the tavern (II.iv.379–491): 'Well thou wilt. . .I do. I will', has often been omitted from stage performances. What was lost by this cutting?

7. 'To be a king and wear a crown is more glorious to them that see it than it is a pleasure to them that wear it.' In what ways is Queen Elizabeth I's saying applicable to Henry IV in this play?

8. Hotspur is 'the only major character in the histories whom it is possible to admire'. 'Hotspur is an engaging barbarian.' Comment on these two views of Hotspur.

9. Choose one passage from each of the groups below, and examine it closely, discussing when relevant its function and importance in the

play, its dramatic effect, its movement, language and imagery.

'My liege I did deny... ...high Majesty.' (I.iii.28–68)
'He never did fall off... ...with revolt.' (I.iii.92–111)
'Peace, cousin... ...half-faced fellowship.' (I.iii.185–206)
'Fie, cousin Percy... ...Christendom.' (III.i.145–62)
'Do not think so... ...of this vow.' (III.ii.129–59)
'O Harry... ...Percy lie.' (V.iv.76–109)

'Peace, good pint pot... ...know not his name.' (II.iv.406–29)
'Bardolph, am I not... ...compass, Sir John.' (III.iii.1–24)
'If I be not ashamed... ...on every hedge.' (IV.ii.11–49)
'Embowelled?... ...come you along with me.' (V.iv.110–28)

You are to direct a performance of *Henry IV Part I*.
Either Write notes for two of the four actors playing Falstaff, Hotspur, Henry IV and Prince Hal; describe the characters and say what effects you wish created from one main speech of each of the two.

OR Choose one of the following episodes and describe how you would stage it, and how you would have the main speeches delivered:

'You were about... ...revolted Mortimer.' (I.iii.21–91)
'Stand!... ...the fat rogue roared!' (II.ii.49–114)
'How now, Kate... ...It must, of force.' (II.iii.36–118)
'Well, thou wilt... ...I do. I will.' (II.iv.379–91)

APPENDIX
SHAKESPEARE'S THEATRE

We should speak, as M.C. Bradbrook reminds us, not of the Elizabethan stage but of Elizabethan stages. Plays of Shakespeare were acted on tour, in the halls of mansions, one at least in Gray's Inn, frequently at Court, and after 1609 at the Blackfriars, a small, roofed theatre for those who could afford the price. But even after his Company acquired the Blackfriars, we know of no play of his not acted (unless, rather improbably, *Troilus* is an exception) for the general public at the Globe, or before 1599 at its predecessor, The Theatre, which, since the Globe was constructed from the same timbers, must have resembled it. Describing the Globe, we can claim therefore to be describing, in an acceptable sense, Shakespeare's theatre, the physical structure his plays were designed to fit. Even in the few probably written for a first performance elsewhere, adaptability to that structure would be in his mind.

For the facilities of the Globe we have evidence from the drawing of the Swan theatre (based on a sketch made by a visitor to London about 1596) which depicts the interior of another public theatre; the builder's contract for the Fortune theatre, which in certain respects (fortunately including the dimensions and position of the stage) was to copy the Globe; indications in the dramatic texts; comments, like Ben Jonson's on the throne let down from above by machinery; and eye-witness testimony to the number of spectators (in round figures, 3000) accommodated in the auditorium.

In communicating with the audience, the actor was most favourably placed. Soliloquising at the centre of the front of the great platform, he was at the mid-point of the theatre, with no one among the spectators more than sixty feet away from him. That platform-stage (Figs I and II) was the most important feature for performance at the Globe. It had the audience – standing in the yard (10) and seated in the galleries (9) – on three sides of it. It was 43 feet wide, and 27½ feet from front to back. Raised (?5½ feet) above the level of the yard, it had a trap-door (II.8)

SHAKESPEARE'S THEATRE

The stage and its adjuncts; the tiring-house; and the auditorium.

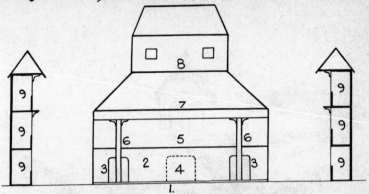

FIG I ELEVATION

1. Platform stage (approximately five feet above the ground) 2. Tiring-house
3. Tiring-house doors to stage 4. Conjectured third door 5. Tiring-house
gallery (balustrade and partitioning not shown) 6. Pillars supporting the
heavens 7. The heavens 8. The hut 9. The spectators' galleries

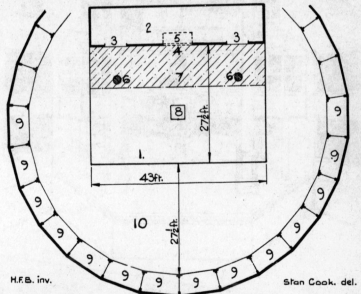

H.F.B. inv.   Stan Cook. del.

FIG II PLAN

1. Platform stage 2. Tiring-house 3. Tiring-house doors to stage
4. Conjectural third door 5. Conjectural discovery space (alternatively behind 3)
6. Pillars supporting the heavens 7. The heavens 8. Trap door 9. Spectators'
gallery 10. The yard

The Globe

An artist's imaginative recreation of a typical Elizabethan theatre

giving access to the space below it. The actors, with their equipment, occupied the 'tiring house' (attiring-house: 2) immediately at the back of the stage. The stage-direction 'within' means inside the tiring-house. Along its frontage, probably from the top of the second storey, juts out the canopy or 'Heavens', carried on two large pillars rising through the platform (6, 7) and sheltering the rear part of the stage, the rest of which, like the yard, was open to the sky. If the 'hut' (I.8), housing the machinery for descents, stood, as in the Swan drawing, above the 'Heavens', that covering must have had a trap-door, so that the descents could be made through it.

Descents are one illustration of the vertical dimension the dramatist could use to supplement the playing-area of the great platform. The other opportunities are provided by the tiring-house frontage or facade. About this facade the evidence is not as complete or clear as we should like, so that Fig. I is in part conjectural. Two doors giving entry to the platform there certainly were (3). A third (4) is probable but not certain. When curtained, a door, most probably this one, would furnish what must be termed a discovery-space (II.5), not an inner stage (on which action in any depth would have been out of sight for a significant part of the audience). Usually no more than two actors were revealed (exceptionally, three), who often then moved out on to the platform. An example of this is Ferdinand and Miranda in *The Tempest* 'discovered' at chess, then seen on the platform speaking with their fathers. Similarly the gallery (I.5) was not an upper stage. Its use was not limited to the actors: sometimes it functioned as 'lords' rooms' for favoured spectators, sometimes, perhaps, as a musician's gallery. Frequently the whole gallery would not be needed for what took place aloft: a window-stage (as in the first balcony scene in *Romeo*, even perhaps in the second) would suffice. Most probably this would be a part (at one end) of the gallery itself; or just possibly, if the gallery did not (as it does in the Swan drawing) extend the whole width of the tiring-house, a window over the left or right-hand door. As the texts show, whatever was presented aloft, or in the discovery-space, was directly related to the action on the platform, so that at no time was there left, between the audience and the action of the drama, a great bare space of platform-stage. In relating Shakespeare's drama to the physical conditions of the theatre, the primacy of that platform is never to be forgotten.

Note: The present brief account owes most to C. Walter Hodges, *The Globe Restored*; Richard Hosley in *A New Companion to Shakespeare Studies*, and in *The Revels History of English Drama*; and to articles by Hosley and Richard Southern in *Shakespeare Survey*, 12, 1959, where full discussion can be found.

HAROLD BROOKS

FURTHER READING

The text used is that of *King Henry IV Part I*, edited by Peter Hollindale (The Macmillan Shakespeare, 1975).

Relevant passages and chapters will be found in the following books:

Shakespeare's life and career

S. Schoenbaum, *William Shakespeare: A Documentary Life* (Oxford: 1975). The definitive life of Shakespeare, reproducing every document having any connection with him, and distinguishing clearly between fact and fancy.

Elizabethan theatre

M. C. Bradbrook, *The Rise of the Common Player* (London, 1962).

C. W. Hodges, *The Globe Restored*, 2nd edn (London, 1968).

J. L. Styan, *Shakespeare's Stagecraft* (Cambridge, 1967).

Sources of 'Henry IV Part I'

G. Bullough, *Narrative and Dramatic Sources of Shakespeare, Vol. III* (London, 1960). Gives all possible sources.

K. Muir, *Sources of Shakespeare's Plays* (Methuen, 1977). Admirable account of the various *Chronicles*, etc.

General criticism

W. H. Auden, 'The Prince's Dog' in *The Dyer's Hand* (London, 1963). 'Way-out' ideas; Falstaff glorified.

C. L. Barber, 'Rule and Misrule in *Henry IV*' in *Shakespeare's Festive Comedy* (Princeton, New Jersey, 1959). Relates Falstaff to English folklore.

A. C. Bradley, 'The Rejection of Falstaff' in *Oxford Lectures on Poetry* (London, 1909). All for Falstaff. Almost sentimental.

L. B. Campbell, *Shakespeare's Histories: Mirrors of Elizabethan Policy*

(San Marino, California, 1947). Scholarly examination of Elizabethan assumptions and background.

H. B. Charlton, *Shakespearian Comedy* (London, 1938). Much prefers this Falstaff to the man of the same name in *The Merry Wives of Windsor*.

G. K. Hunter (ed.), *Henry IV Parts I and II* (Macmillan Casebooks: London, 1970). Very useful anthology, containing much of Auden, Barber, Bradley, Charlton, Morgann and Wilson.

S. Johnson, *Johnson on Shakespeare* (Oxford, 1908: many reprintings). Superbly direct and full of common sense.

M. Morgann, *Essay on the Dramatic Character of Sir John Falstaff* (1777). Fierce defence of Falstaff as no coward.

J. Palmer, *Political Characters of Shakespeare* (London, 1945). Interesting to compare this Falstaff with that of Morgann.

M. M. Reese, *The Cease of Majesty* (London, 1961). Outstandingly good on the histories and their Elizabethan background.

G. B. Shaw, *Dramatic Opinions* (London, 1906). A period piece.

E. M. W. Tillyard, *Shakespeare's Histories* (London, 1944). Rather over-simplified. Supports Hal.

D. Traversi, *Shakespeare from Richard II to Henry V* (London, 1957). Examines the play in great detail, as reading matter.

B. Vickers, *The Artistry of Shakespeare's Prose* (London, 1968). Detailed analysis of several passages.

J. Dover Wilson, *The Fortunes of Falstaff* (London, 1953). Very full and searching criticism.

Mastering English Literature

Richard Gill

Mastering English Literature will help readers both to enjoy English Literature and to be successful in 'O' levels, 'A' levels and other public exams. It is an introduction to the study of poetry, novels and drama which helps the reader in four ways – by providing ways of approaching literature, by giving examples and practice exercises, by offering hints on how to write about literature, and by the author's own evident enthusiasm for the subject. With extracts from more than 200 texts, this is an enjoyable account of how to get the maximum satisfaction out of reading, whether it be for formal examinations or simply for pleasure.

Work Out English Literature ('A' level)

S.H. Burton

This book familiarises 'A' level English Literature candidates with every kind of test which they are likely to encounter. Suggested answers are worked out step by step and accompanied by full author's commentary. The book helps students to clarify their aims and establish techniques and standards so that they can make appropriate responses to similar questions when the examination pressures are on. It opens up fresh ways of looking at the full range of set texts, authors and critical judgements and motivates students to know more of these matters.